KW-052-035

TEACH YOURSELF BOOKS

TRANSLATING

IAN F. FINLAY, M.A., F.I.L., F.R.S.A., A.I.Inf.Sc.

TEACH YOURSELF BOOKS

ST PAUL'S HOUSE WARWICK LANE LONDON EC4

First printed 1971

Copyright © 1971
The English Universities Press Limited

ISBN 0 340 12468 7

Printed and bound in Great Britain for
The English Universities Press Ltd
by T. & A. Constable Ltd.,
Hopetoun Street, Edinburgh

TEACH YOURSELF BOOKS

TRANSLATING

Although translators have existed at all times, it is only in the last fifty years or so that they have begun to emerge as a distinct, full-time professional group of practitioners of their art and craft.

This book traces the major developments in translating over the centuries and presents a detailed picture of present-day techniques in the information and publication spheres and deals with various specialized types of translation work. Finally, it includes a section on translator training and practical aids, both to the translator and those who use his services.

"I think it is excellent. It is thorough, complete, readable and very practical. I shall refer many enquirers to this. I have, in fact, learnt from it more than I care to admit."

G. Humphrey Smith
Secretary, The Institute of Linguists

CONTENTS

PREFACE

This book sets out to examine the world of translating from two points of view. Firstly, it seeks to describe briefly what might be called the *status ante*, i.e. the history of translating, and the *status quo*, i.e. the present-day picture in the world of translating. These sections will perhaps be of greater interest to the general reader who wants to know what translators have done in the past and what they are doing now, rather than how they set about doing it. Secondly, the book sets out to explain the precise position of translating amongst the various linguistic activities and to take the reader, as it were, into the translator's office or study and illustrate how he sets to work.

Translating is both a craft and an art, that is to say it involves an accurate and controlled manipulation of language, tempered by a degree of freedom, imagination and creativeness. The purely linguistic background required by the translator as a craftsman can, within limits, be fairly easily acquired or taught, while the purely creative element in his make-up cannot, at least to the same extent, although it can of course be nurtured, guided and developed.

The relatively recent emergence of the translator as a member of a distinct and fairly clear-cut profession means that he has not as yet attained, either within his own ranks or in relation to those who use his services, the position of familiarity shared by his professional colleagues who may be doctors, dentists, lawyers or accountants. There is, consequently, still much confusion, even amongst linguists, about the translator and what he does. On the other hand, there has never been a time in the history of man when translation has been more necessary. During the past few years there has been a vast explosion in virtually every branch of literature and in virtually every language. To take but one example, representative of many, a volume published in Germany in 1968 listing translations from German into English carried out between 1948 and 1964 has over five hundred pages and shows that in 1966, for example, nearly 4,000 books were translated from and nearly 4,500 into German, and this kind of picture is being repeated, to a greater or lesser extent, all over the world. It has been estimated in the scientific and technical sphere that half the world's scientists cannot read half the world's scientific literature purely because it is in languages that they do not understand. Consequently, the translator is in the latter half of the twentieth century an essential agent acting as a mediator across the language barrier in a wide number of fields. It is also unlikely that his importance will diminish even bearing in mind the growing number of people acquiring for themselves a reading knowledge of languages within their own subject-fields.

It is, therefore, hoped that this volume will serve to cast some light on translating and to dispel some of the confusion and misconceptions that surround it, so that those who have read it will come away with a broad, yet fairly detailed picture of the world of the translator.

Although the book has been written predominantly with English conditions in mind, it does include several references to continental practices and those in other parts of the world and, unlike the law, the art and craft of translating do not suffer unduly on being transplanted from one country or continent to another.

Although the number of books devoted specifically to translating is fairly small—much of the relevant literature being tucked away in various specialized journals—the works in the following list will be found useful in that they present an authoritative picture of various facets of the subject. Likewise, the reading lists at the end of the various chapters will give the reader an opportunity to pursue matters in greater detail.

READING LIST

Brower, R. A. (editor)—*On Translation*. New York, 1966.
Cary, E.—*La traduction dans le monde moderne*. Geneva, 1965.
Feidel, G.—*Technische Texte richtig übersetzen*. Düsseldorf and Vienna, 1970.
Finch, C. A.—*An Approach to Technical Translation*. London, 1969.
Mounin, G.—*Les problèmes théoretiques de la traduction*. Paris, 1963.
Savory, T.—*The Art of Translation*. London, 1968.
Tarnóczi, L.—*Fordítókalauz*. Budapest, 1966.
Unesco—*Scientific and Technical Translating*. Paris, 1957.

CHAPTER I

TRANSLATING, ITS NATURE AND CRITERIA

What is translation, and what principles are involved in translating? It is these and related matters that we shall be considering in this chapter.

A translation may be defined as a presentation of a text in a language other than that in which it was originally written. The word "written" should be stressed, since it distinguishes translating from the start from interpreting, which may be defined as the presentation of a statement in a language other than that in which it was originally spoken. Herein lies the basic difference between translating and interpreting. Translating is concerned with the conversion of the written word, interpreting with that of the spoken word. As with most related disciplines, there are varieties of translating, such as oral translating, i.e. the reading aloud of a text in a language other than that in which it is written, or monitoring, i.e. the extraction of relevant information from a radio broadcast in a foreign language, which verge on the normal territory of interpreting. The two disciplines of translating and interpreting are, however, normally quite separate and are, in fact, relatively rarely practised to the same degree of ability by one and the same person. It has been said, with more than a grain of truth, that the translator is perhaps ideally of an introvert temperament, while the interpreter is perhaps ideally of an extrovert temperament, without the implication that either is neurotic! Another useful analogy is to liken the translator to the solicitor and the interpreter to the barrister. The one carries out most of his work within the confines of his office, while the other appears before the public in an assembly hall or court. Both nevertheless have their places in the linguistic and legal world respectively, but that place, function and probably temperament differ.

The need for a translation arises when a person wishes to know the contents of a document written in a language he does not know. In other words, the language of the original forms a barrier to his understanding of it, and the services of a translator are called in to bridge that barrier or gap.

This causes us to ask what the person requiring the translation expects of it or, in other words, why he wants it and what criteria he is likely to apply when judging the translation. Although opinions have differed at various times as to what is a good translation and although, as we shall be seeing later, the criteria may differ slightly depending on the purpose for which the translation is required, there are amongst translators certain fairly well-defined characteristics of a good translation, even if the relative stress placed on them may occasionally be subject to discussion.

Normally, it is universally accepted that any translation worthy of the name must reproduce the full sense of the original, omitting nothing and adding nothing. If it does either of these things, then it is no longer a translation, but moves into the spheres of the summary, précis, adaptation, version, abstract or arrangement. The word "sense" implies both the innate meaning and the fact that this meaning is presented in a way that is fully intelligible. The "sense" is, therefore, "intelligible meaning". Ideally, the translation should give the sense of the original in such a way that the reader is unaware that he is reading a translation. Thus, to paraphrase a saying by Oscar Wilde, the art of the translator is to conceal the translation or to conceal the act or art of translation. All traces of the original text should, as it were, disappear, and a new original appear in its place, without there being any sign of an intermediate process of transition. The reader should experience the same impression as if he were reading, let us say, a document in English about nuclear physics, rather than a document about nuclear physics that he will be only too well aware has been translated, even if he does not know from what language.

So far, we have asked of our translator a knowledge of the original language, such that he can understand fully on the linguistic level what the original author meant, coupled with a full understanding of the subject-matter of the original text, in this case a full understanding of matters concerned with nuclear physics. In order that the reader may not be aware that he is reading a translation, it is also necessary that the translator should have genuine facility and ease of expression in the language into which he is translating, being able to express the thoughts of the original easily in the new linguistic medium. As we shall see later, the translator can by no means always count on being given a well-written original from which to work— scientists, in particular, often being notoriously bad writers, not only in English, but also in other languages. Foolish as it may sound, it is, therefore, quite possible that a translation can be better than the original from which it was prepared, even if this remark is not perhaps excessively apposite when applied to the translations of Shakespeare's plays into German!

It might be useful at this stage to introduce two fairly recent terms often encountered in texts relating to translating. These are the terms "source language" and "target language". The former is the language from which a translation is made, while the latter is the language into which a translation is made.

In addition to his perfect and up-to-date knowledge of

the source language, his full understanding of the subject-matter of the text in the source language, a knowledge of the equivalent terminology in the target language, and facility of expression therein, the translator must also have an appreciation of and feeling for different styles, tones, nuances and registers in both the source and target languages, this assisting him in recreating the mood of the original in his translation. Needless to say, this latter facility is of much greater importance in literary translations than in those of a technical or scientific character.

Finally, the translator should see to it that his final translation is presented in an acceptable form. Too often translators produce good work that is marred by poor presentation. Ideally, all translations should be produced in a form suitable for direct presentation to a printer, whether they are intended for publication or not. It is a poor excuse on the part of any translator to say "I'm a translator, not a typist".

These then are the main criteria by which a translation should be judged. They can be summed up by saying that the translation should ideally make the same impression on a native-speaker of the target language who is conversant with the subject-matter of the original as the original did on the native-speaker of the source language. In other words, an English doctor should be able to read a translation of a paper on leukaemia, which has been translated from French, and receive the same impression of complete correctness and conviction as did one of his French colleagues reading the original. Thus we see that the translator begins to emerge on a par with the original author, the only difference being that the material he is processing was presented to him in a foreign language, he having recreated it, as it were, in the target language. An analogy from the world of music might be that someone hearing the orchestral version of Mussorgsky's "Pictures from an Exhibition", prepared by Ravel, would be unaware that the work had originally been written for the piano. Likewise, a comparison between a poor and good translation of the same text will very quickly reveal that translation is very much more than a pure craft.

These criteria can best be achieved if certain qualities are present in the translator. Equally well, the criteria assume varying degrees of importance, depending on the purpose for which the translation is being made. We shall now consider these two points.

In order that a translation should read as an original composition, it is highly desirable, even if not absolutely essential in all cases, that it should be made by someone who is translating into his or her mother tongue. Stated in another way, it is the general consensus of opinion amongst professional translators in this country that translators should, unless bilingual (bearing in mind all that this implies), translate solely into their mother tongue or, to use a term that is fast gaining acceptance as being a more accurate description, their "language of habitual use". Another possible term is "language of adoption".

Facility in the use of language is a very intimate component of our make-up and, unlike many skills and abilities that we acquire in the course of our lives, it is something which is, with rare exceptions, acquired in relation to one language only. Although it is possible to analyse to a certain extent the process of thought and linguistic expression resulting from it, the process is in many ways akin to a conditioned reflex and to that degree involuntary. Consequently, it is rarely likely that one person will develop two sets of conditioned reflexes which apply with equal facility to two different, often highly unrelated languages, and it is also pretty certain that the later in life the second language is grafted on to a person, the less well he or she will master it in all its aspects. It would be fatuous to suggest that, let us say, a university course lasting three or four years could produce a degree of facility and conditioned reflexes in a language comparable to those acquired in the mother tongue which has been one's sole means of linguistic expression for the first and most impressionable years of one's life. The chameleon is far more efficient at visual adaptation than most human beings are at linguistic adaptation, and their general ability thereat normally varies inversely as their age.

There have been rare exceptions to this, for example, Joseph Conrad, born J. Konrad Korzeniowski with Polish as his native language, who wrote in, but did not translate into, considerably better English than most of us can produce as our mother tongue. Nevertheless, such exceptions tend only to prove the rule that translating out of one's language of habitual use is something to be avoided, in addition to which it is usually quite unnecessary, since with little effort it is possible to find a translator of the necessary mother tongue. The printed word bristles with examples of what can happen when people translate out of their mother tongue, ranging from the merely quaint or amusing to the grotesque, obscene and even damaging and fatal. Beware, therefore, of those translators who claim that they can or will translate from and into several languages on virtually any subject. Look rather for the translator who undertakes to translate from various foreign languages into his mother tongue or language of adoption within a fairly closely circumscribed sphere of subjects. It is only fair to point out here that translating into a foreign language can be and is an excellent exercise for testing one's understanding of the structure of that foreign language. It is, however, as such that it should be indulged in, not as a professional activity.

This brings us to another point amongst the criteria for a good translation, i.e. that it should not read as a translation since the correct terms will have been used for the concepts involved. This criterion is, of course, of paramount importance when we come to consider subject-matter of a technical or specialized nature, particularly if it is intended for instructional or promotional publication. The days of the universal geniuses have passed as have those, for the most part, of the cultivated amateur, and there is today an increasing demand for the person who knows more and more about less and less, in other words, the expert in a given, usually quite narrow, subject. Regrettable as this may be, particularly when it involves excessively early specialization in secondary education, it is a fact of the world in which we live and in which we have to earn our livings. The translator of technical material must be conversant with and able to understand that material. In other words, he must be able to understand it in the source language and able to transfer it intelligibly, by using the correct terminology, into the target language. He must know, for example, the occasions on which it is correct to use one of such seemingly synonymous words as "roll", "roller", "wheel" or "disc". He must know, for example, that although the Germans speak of the interval of a "pure fifth" in music the English term is "perfect fifth". When a dictionary offers a number of alternative translations for a given term in a foreign language, it is unlikely that more than one of them will be correct or appropriate in a given context. Many dictionaries offer no assistance in this direction, so that a knowledge of the subject-matter on the part of the translator is essential if he is to progress beyond the stage of guessing or using his intuition, these both being very unreliable methods for arriving at a correct solution in a given case.

The realization of the need to understand what one is translating has given rise to certain more vocationally oriented courses of training for translators which have been established in recent years, these combining linguistic and technical knowledge in certain spheres. We shall have more to say about these courses later. It is, in fact, this combination of linguistic and subject-matter knowledge that is an essential part of the equipment of the technical translator, this being why such translators state the languages from which and the subjects on which they translate into their mother tongue or language of habitual use.

We have, on several occasions, referred to languages (plural) from which people translate into their mother tongue (singular). There is a very good reason for this. It is quite possible and by no means unusual for a translator to know a number of different foreign languages well enough to translate from them into his mother tongue material on his special subject(s). This is, firstly, because the subject-matter will be a common factor to all the texts in the various source languages and, secondly, because there is one target language only which the translator can handle with full facility because it will be his language of habitual use. Although most translators will, partly for reasons of training and partly for psychological reasons, tend to be happiest when translating from a given source language, many can translate from two or three, while there are a few who can translate from up to five, very few being able to translate from up to ten or more. Usually, however, the greater the number of languages translated from, the smaller will be the number of subjects involved. Conversely, the smaller the number of languages translated from, the larger will tend to be the number of subjects involved. To adopt a personal note, my own best foreign language is Dutch, while the subject with which I am possibly most conversant is synthetic fibre technology. Whereas I can translate from Dutch into English material in a fairly wide range of subjects, I can translate from, let us say, Spanish and Danish, solely material relating to synthetic fibre technology. Dutch is the language in which I approach, but do not reach, bilinguality, whereas I am literate in Spanish and Danish merely in the sphere of synthetic fibre technology.

It is useful, in this context, for translators to carry out from time to time what one might call a private language audit, listing in order the nature of their knowledge of various languages. This will normally range from the mother tongue, via languages they know to varying degrees, down to those they can merely identify. There will usually too be those that they cannot even identify, bearing in mind the large number of languages in the world. Parts of the Bible, for example, have been translated into more than eleven hundred different languages or dialects!

Another point worth mentioning in this context is that the translator from languages such as French, German and Russian can afford to specialize to a very much greater extent than, let us say, the translator from Finnish or Japanese. The reason for this is that there are far fewer people who can translate from Finnish or Japanese into English, particularly in technical spheres, than there are who can carry out such work from French, German and Russian. Consequently, the former have to be much more omnivorous in their subject-matter diet than their possibly vegetarian colleagues working from the more common or better-known languages. On the other hand, as we shall be seeing later, rarity value can bring its financial rewards in the world of translating.

Returning to the criterion relating to ease and facility of expression in the target language, we must now consider two different categories of translations, since this criterion plays an important role, albeit of varying intensity, in them. There are basically two types of translations defined by the purpose for which they are intended. These are translations required either for information or publication.

Let us consider each of these categories in turn and the criteria to be applied to them. The majority of translations of correspondence and scientific or technical material required by British industry will, for example, be needed primarily for the information contained therein. Such translations will be intended to provide answers to such questions as: "When can this firm supply the equipment we require?" —"Is this new method for preparing sulphuric acid likely to affect our position in the market?"—"Does this new Dutch patent application infringe our process?"—"Do we need to send a technical expert to Tunis to sort out this processing difficulty or will a copy of Note 345 tell them all they need to know?" Most such translations will in fact be from a variety of foreign languages into English. They will be required quickly and once the information they contain has been assimilated and acted upon, they will quite quickly lose their value. In other words, the information obtained from them has a fairly short and limited useful life. They may in this respect be compared to daily newspapers, much of the information in which is ephemeral rather than permanent in value. Such information translations have, in most cases, to be prepared quickly, but must at the same time be completely accurate and reliable. On the other hand, since they are being read for the information they contain, not so much attention is or need be paid to ease of reading, stylistic matters and the like as in the case of the second basic category of translations, i.e. those intended for publication in one form or another.

These include, for example, translations of books and articles, technical sales literature, publicity and promotional literature and advertisements and sales aids of various types. Much of this latter material will, in Great Britain, be required to be translated from English into the languages of the countries to which the goods they refer to are being exported. Thus, apart from books which are translated into English for sale on the English-speaking market, the bulk of publication translations will consist of literature intended to inform people of our products and goods or of our tourist attractions. It is essential that such translations should meet a requirement which is not perhaps so important in information translations. The former material was, as it were, passive and static, while this latter material is active and dynamic, or at least should be, in that it has to take its place with other similar material in a highly competitive market. It is necessary that such material be translated perfectly from the point of view of terminology, that it should be stylistically immaculate and that it should incorporate the correct vocabulary and be set at the proper level for the audience to which it is directed—which will be an audience in the 1970's, not one of the mid-twenties. Equally well, it would be inadvisable to insert the same advertisement in a paper read mainly by teenagers as in that read by company directors.

Publication translations of this type must be able to be placed on a par with, for example, sales literature produced in the country to which they are being sent. Thus, a German who is thinking of buying a new car must be able to study the sales literature of the manufacturer of a local Volkswagen or Opel and compare it with that relating to a Volvo, Jaguar or Renault and not be aware at any stage that the one is locally produced, while the others are produced in Sweden, Great Britain or France respectively. Seen in this light, the importance of our statement about not translating out of one's language of habitual use will be evident, since it is unlikely that the non-native-speaker will be able to acquire just that sense of what the Germans call *Sprachgefühl* or feeling for what is correct in a language, particularly in the psychologically subtle world of advertising and hidden persuading.

Various other important points arise in connexion with such publication translations, certain of which amount virtually to exercises in copy-writing. Firstly, it should be remembered that, although German, for example, is the official language of Germany (West and East) and Austria and is one of the four official languages in Switzerland, the German spoken and used in these four territories is by no means the same. Those who doubt this would do well to look at equivalent patent specifications granted in these countries when it will very likely be found that one and the same technical term in, let us say, English will have been translated in four different ways, one for each of the countries using German. This is particularly so in the case of modern technical terms which have not yet found their way into standard dictionaries or works of reference. For this reason alone, there is much to be said for having separate literature produced for every country, irrespective of whether it has the same language as other countries. After all, it was Bernard Shaw, I think, who said that England and America were two countries separated by the same language! On the more prosaic and naïve plane, it should also be remembered that there are no such languages as, for example, Belgian or Peruvian. Belgium is officially bilingual in relation to French and Flemish (Dutch), while Spanish is the language of Peru, albeit not in every respect the same Spanish as is used and spoken in Spain itself. Talking of South America, it should also be remembered that Portuguese is the language of Brazil, she being alone in this respect amongst the South and Central American republics.

Secondly, countries differ not only in relation to language, but also in relation to habits, psychology, prejudices and the like. Consequently, a direct translation of a publicity leaflet or advertisement which has proved eminently suitable and successful, let us say, in England will by no means necessarily be equally appropriate in, let us say, France or Pakistan. There are cases in which certain living creatures, shapes or colours may be taboo in various countries or contexts. This is, therefore, one reason why all such material should preferably be prepared or at least checked in the country in which it is to be used, since otherwise grave errors may be committed, more often than not quite innocently or unwittingly. Trade marks too cannot always be transported unchallenged from one country to another.

There have been several occasions on which firms have lived to regret not checking with native-speakers the connotations of a given trade mark in a given language. It is all very well to make sure that a word is free for registration in a given country, but it is also wise to establish that this freedom may not reside in its social lack of acceptability there! It sometimes also happens that firms cannot trade under their own name in certain countries because of unfortunate associations it may have in the vernaculars. It should perhaps also be pointed out that in some cases parts of advertisements for use in foreign countries are not translated because a judicious sprinkling of English or American words adds a certain snob appeal to them. A glance at some newspapers and magazines from Germany, France or the Netherlands will confirm this. It is also an interesting fact that in the latter country most brands of cigarettes have English or American names, while nearly all brands of cigars have Dutch names.

The preparation of publicity material in foreign languages is really something deserving of a chapter, if not a book to itself. Although we cannot do this here, it is perhaps worth pointing out the importance of qualified proofreading of all foreign-language material that may be set and printed by English printers. There have been many occasions on which firms have found, often at the last minute, that because of inadequate or inexpert proofreading expensively produced literature could not be used abroad for the intended purpose. Missing words, words spelt incorrectly, omitted accents or other signs, words split incorrectly, the incorrect use of capital letters—these and many other things can easily mar the appearance of and impression given by a text, all because of neglecting proof-reading. It will, in fact, be found that most linguistic errors arise through ignorance or the under-estimation of the problems involved on the part of those with no linguistic training or appreciation. We shall later be having more to say about this matter which might be called "customer education".

Because of the greater degree of polish they require and also because they are ideally prepared in the country in which they are to be used, publicity translations normally take longer to prepare than information translations. They likewise cost more, but their cost of production is always but a small fraction of the total cost of the project or campaign of which they form part. For example, I recently heard of a case in which a short letter translated from English into French—costing a few shillings—had resulted in little less than a million pounds worth of business!

Finally, let us consider briefly desirable qualities that a translator should have if he is to be successful in his chosen profession. We have already considered the reasons for most of these and those for the others will become apparent later in the book.

The translator must have an excellent, up-to-date knowledge of his source languages, full facility in the handling of his target language, which will be his mother tongue or language of habitual use, and a knowledge and understanding of the latest subject-matter in his fields of specialization. This is, as it were, his professional equipment. In addition to this, it is desirable that he should have an enquiring mind, wide interests, a good memory, the ability to grasp quickly the basic principles of new developments. He should be willing to work on his own, often at high speeds, but should be humble enough to consult others should his own knowledge not always prove adequate to the task in hand. He should be able to type fairly quickly and accurately and, if he is working mainly for publication, should have more than a nodding acquaintance with printing techniques and proof-reading. If he is working basically as an information translator, let us say, for an industrial firm, he should have the flexibility of mind to enable him to switch rapidly from one source language to another as well as from one subject-matter to another since, as we shall be seeing, this ability is frequently required of him in such work. Bearing in mind the nature of the translator's work, i.e. the processing of the written word, it is, strictly speaking, unnecessary that he should be able to speak the languages he is dealing with. If he does speak them, it is an advantage rather than a hindrance, but this skill is in many ways a luxury that he can dispense with. It is, however, desirable that he should have an approximate idea about the pronunciation of his source languages, even if this is restricted to knowing how proper names and place names are pronounced. The same applies to an ability to write his source languages. If he can, well and good, if he cannot, it does not matter. There are many other skills and qualities that are much more desirable in a translator as will be apparent from what has been said earlier in this chapter.

Added to all the qualities mentioned, he must also have a full knowledge of the literary aids available within his language and subject-matter specializations. These include dictionaries, grammars, reference books, technical literature and the like. This knowledge should also, if possible, extend to the various mechanical aids available to him, such as typewriters, tape recorders, photocopying machines, etc. Finally, the translator should also seek to belong to the professional organizations provided for him, in order that he should have regular opportunities to meet his colleagues and discuss experiences and problems with them.

READING LIST

Bäse, H.-J.—*Was ist ein Fachübersetzer?* Babel, Vol. XIV, No. 2, 1967, pp. 77-84.

Cook-Radmore, D. A. J.—*What is a Translation?* Institute of Linguists, London, 1964.

Finlay, I. F.—*The Translation Profession in England—its Nature and Organization.* Anuvad, November 1965, pp. 85-96.

Newmark, P.—*Some Notes on Translation and Translators*.
The Incorporated Linguist, October 1969, pp. 79-85.

Suchodolski, P.—*The Quality, Training and Professional
Status of the Technical Translator*. The Incorporated
Linguist, January 1962, pp. 17-22.

Weis, E.—*Translation—a Profession*. Babel, Vol. XIII, No.
1, 1967, pp. 14-22.

CHAPTER II

TRANSLATING IN THE PAST

The art of the translator is an ancient one, even if not quite as old as that of the interpreter, who can pride himself on at least one specific biblical reference as well as the symbolic account of the building of the Tower of Babel which, in fact, caused the very confusion of tongues it was calculated to avoid. The art of the interpreter also predates that of the translator in that the former processes the spoken word while the latter is called upon only when it is a question of the written word. The spoken word came very much earlier than the written word in the case of most languages. The Japanese, for example, had a spoken language for several centuries before they adopted the Chinese method of writing in the first centuries after the birth of Christ. There are still today many languages spoken by small groups of people in remote parts of the world which have never been properly codified or written down, so that the question of translating from them does not arise.

A history of translating must of necessity become a history of mankind in the widest sense and, in the narrower sense, of the interaction between peoples of different languages via the written word. I say written rather than printed word for, although the invention of printing in Europe, in about the middle of the fifteenth century, gave a remarkable impetus to the spread of the written word, being in this way possibly the greatest invention of all times, translating obviously preceded its development and was practised for centuries by hand. It should also be remembered in this context that it was not until the latter half of the nineteenth century that the typewriter became to any extent a sophisticated and reasonably common object.

It will in this short chapter be possible merely to refer to some of the outstanding landmarks in the long and venerable history of translating, stressing the part that has been played by those who were not monolingual in the transfer of knowledge and experience from one cultural sphere to another. A little reflexion will show that we should be much the poorer if we were from tomorrow to be bereft of all books that had not originally been written in English, for example. We should immediately lose access to the Bible, the Odyssey, the Iliad, the Divine Comedy, Don Quixote, Faust, the plays of such authors as Molière, Racine, Strindberg and Ibsen, the majority of the world's greatest songs and operas, not to mention all the literature of the Far and Middle East. This can be said even bearing in mind that the contribution of the English-speaking peoples to the arts has, without doubt, been greatest in the field of literature, supreme greatness in music, painting and architecture having been reserved for such countries as Germany, Italy and France.

It will be convenient to begin our brief survey of the history of translating in ancient Greek times when that country was undisputedly the centre of western civilization. Two movements in translating developed from Greece. The first of these was concerned with translations made from Greek into Latin, the earliest literary translation, that of Homer's *Odyssey* into Latin by Livius Andronicus, having been made about 250 B.C. Fragments of this early example of the translator's art still survive. The Latin authors Catullus and Cicero were frequent translators from Greek into Latin and, with the rise in importance of Rome as the centre of a great empire, there was also a certain amount of translating from Latin into Greek. It is interesting to note that, even at this very early stage, famous literary figures in their own right were attracted by the challenge that is always offered by translating. This is a phenomenon that characterizes the art down through the centuries.

Moving into the early centuries of the Christian era, we find that there was in the eighth and ninth centuries a marked rise in the development of Arabian learning, and it was this that gave rise to the other movement in the direction of translations from Greek. The majority of early developments in Arabian scholarship was based on Greek knowledge which was made available in Arabic for the most part by Syrian scholars who came to Baghdad where they translated the works of such Greek scholars as Aristotle, Plato, Galen, Hippocrates and others into Arabic. Their activity was such that Baghdad became at that time virtually the centre of a school of translation.

The Moorish invasion of Spain took place in the eighth century and, as a result of it, these Arabic texts found their way to Toledo in the eleventh and twelfth century, where another school of translators was soon engaged in converting the Arabic texts into Latin, which was then the *lingua franca* in the world of learning. In certain cases, one and the same text may have turned full circle as it were, having been translated from the original Latin into Greek and then into Arabic, eventually to be translated back into Latin again. Such double and triple translations frequently suffered greatly in accuracy in the process, as has been shown by many a simple after-dinner game of asking people of various mother tongues to translate a sentence from a foreign source language into their mother tongue. It is often found that, on completing the circle, the final version is quite different from its parent. Such double translations are however still carried out quite often today. For example, if a work in an obscure language has been translated into a better known language, this latter version will frequently be used as the source for translations into other languages, emerging as it were as a new original, sometimes of course suffering greatly in the process.

One of the principal translators working in Toledo during the twelfth century, Gerard of Cremona (1114-1187), has in fact come to be regarded as the patron saint of translators. During his years in Toledo he was responsible for translating a wide variety of scientific works in Greek and Arabic into Latin.

Toledo was for more than a century a centre of attraction for many scholars from different countries, including Adelard of Bath, an English scholastic philosopher, who had studied in France and travelled in Spain, Italy, north Africa and Asia Minor. One of his best-known translations was that of Euclid's *Elements* into Latin, probably from an Arabic version. By about 1200, copies of the original Greek works were beginning to reach Toledo, and the desirability of translating them rather than using the Arabic translations began to be felt. By the end of the twelfth century, the art of translation had reached heights that have seldom been equalled, let alone surpassed. It needs little imagination to realize the great achievements of these early translators, working under primitive conditions and without facilities that would be considered normal today. Apart from scientific works, most translations at this time were of religious works. Mention of religious works serves to remind us that translations of the Bible into various vernaculars have throughout the history of translating occupied an important place. Such translations were often a vehicle for codifying a language and giving rise to a generally accepted literary form of it. This was the case with the translation of the Bible into High German made by Martin Luther during the first half of the sixteenth century.

Another unifying and purifying influence on certain languages was the setting up of academies, part of whose function it was to decide on proper linguistic usage. These academies were very much a fruit of the Renaissance. One of the most famous, still in existence today, was the *Académie française*, founded in 1635. Similar bodies in Spain and Italy have also played an important role in establishing linguistic standards and thus, indirectly, providing translators with part of the equipment needed for practising their profession effectively. Even today, translating from many languages is greatly hampered because of the lack of a standard language or adequate dictionaries.

The first great age of translating in England was that of Elizabeth I. It is quite astonishing how many translations were made during the latter half of the sixteenth century in England, mainly from languages such as Greek, Latin, French, Italian and Spanish. Certain of these involved the "double translation" principle already referred to above in so far as works which had originally been written in Latin or Greek were translated into English from the French versions. Another interesting phenomenon which is still to be encountered in the world of literary translating is the number of different translations that was made and is in fact still being made of various classical works. There have been countless translations, not only into English, but also into a variety of other languages, of the great Greek and Latin classics as well as of later great works from the literatures of European countries. Any translation is a challenge and an exercise in communication, but attempts to translate, let us say, Homer's *Odyssey* or *Iliad* never cease to attract translators. The perennial appeal of these and other works partly of course resides in the universal message they convey.

Another interesting point is that, whereas we sometimes have to wait several decades today before a translation into English is made of some modern work of outstanding importance, there was in the sixteenth and seventeenth century often very little time between the appearance of a foreign original and its translation into English. One thinks in this

context, for example, of John Florio's translation of
Montaigne's *Essays*, made in 1603, the original French
having appeared in 1580, and of Thomas Shelton's translation of Cervantes' *Don Quixote*, which appeared in 1612,
only seven years after the original Spanish.

During the seventeenth century, it was still for the most
part the Greek and Latin classics that attracted the attention
of translators in England. John Dryden's translations of
Juvenal (1693) and Virgil (1697) come into this category.
It should, incidentally, be noted that much useful information on translating techniques can be gleaned from the
introductions to many of these early translations of the
classics. An interesting document in this context is the Earl
of Roscommon's *An Essay on Translated Verse* which appeared in London in 1684.

The translations of Alexander Pope and William Cowper
belong to the eighteenth century, these once again including
translations of the *Odyssey* and *Iliad*. It was also in this
century that the German translations of these works by
J. H. Voss (1751-1826) appeared. Comparison of the
various English and these German translations is instructive. The famous translations into German of Shakespeare's
plays by August Wilhelm von Schlegel (1767-1845) also
belong to the end of the eighteenth and beginning of the
nineteenth century, as do those into German of Cervantes'
Don Quixote and various works by Elizabethan dramatists
by Johann Ludwig Tieck (1773-1853). Of interest from the
point of view of the criteria of a good translation was
Alexander Fraser Tytler, Lord Woodhouselee's *Essay on
the Principles of Translation*, which appeared in 1790. It
was he who stated that a good translation is that in which
the merit of the original work is so completely transfused
into another language, as to be distinctly apprehended, and
as strongly felt, by a native of the country to which that
language belongs, as it is by those who speak the language
of the original work. This important work by a professor

of history at Edinburgh is still worth reading, particularly for the many annotated examples of translations into English of the classics which he gives. Comparison of the above description of a good translation with what was said on this subject in Chapter I will show that there has been little change in the criteria applied.

Translators have at times been involved in the deciphering of ancient manuscripts or documents, this aspect of their work serving to surround them with a certain degree of glamour on the part of the general public. One such example was the key for the decipherment of the ancient monuments of Egypt provided by the so-called Rosetta stone. It was found near Fort Julien, about 4 miles north of the town of Rosetta in 1799 by Boussard, a French officer. It consisted of a basalt stele inscribed in hieroglyphic, demotic and Greek with a decree of the priests assembled at Memphis in favour of Ptolemy V. Epiphanes. The deciphering was due to the French orientalist Jean-François Champollion (1790-1832). The Rosetta stone was ceded to the English at the capitulation of Alexandria in 1801 and is now one of the most prized exhibits in the British Museum in London.

Moving into the nineteenth century proper, we find that the spectrum of languages from which works were translated into English widened considerably compared with earlier centuries, although there was still a goodly representation of the classics. It must also be remembered that this was the century *par excellence* of missionaries in various parts of the world, the activities of whom were to bring as a fringe benefit as it were, the translation of the whole or parts of the Bible into an amazing variety of languages and dialects, these often being the first examples of written forms of some of these previously solely oral means of communication. The importance of missionaries in the linguistic sphere should never be under-estimated. Many valuable works on Japanese and Chinese, for example, were

B

prepared by missionaries. Such work is still continuing today in many remoter parts of the world.

In the purely literary sphere Thomas Carlyle (1795-1881) emerges as an important nineteenth century translator. It was in 1824 that he translated Goethe's *Wilhelm Meister* into English. This century also saw the production of many translations by poets, often of verse into verse. Examples by Shelley, Byron and the American Longfellow abound. Another famous translation was that by Edward Fitzgerald of the *Rubaiyat* of Omar Khayyám. This was from Persian, although Fitzgerald also made successful translations from Spanish and ancient Greek. It is interesting in this context to reflect that many works originating in the Middle East and Asia were first translated into English, while those of Russian origin reached Europe through French, the works of many Scandinavian authors, particularly those from Sweden, first attracting the attention of German translators.

A highly instructive nineteenth-century document about translation is Matthew Arnold's essay *On Translating Homer* which appeared in 1861. Arnold's main thesis was that a translation should affect us in the same way as the original may have been supposed to have affected its first readers. This essay was written as a criticism of a translation of Homer made by F. W. Newman, the brother of Cardinal Newman. Newman believed in verbal exactitude rather than preservation of an aesthetic effect, hence the controversy between him and Arnold. Although the material with which most modern translators have to deal is very different from the classical Greek of Homer, there is much to be learnt from studying such exchanges by skilled translators of the past. After all, there are many present-day disciplines not having the benefit of such an illustrious past history which has very largely been preserved for us.

Towards the end of the nineteenth century there were many translations into English from languages which had hitherto been virtually a closed book to English readers. There were translations of several of the many novels by the Hungarian author M. Jókai (1825-1904), while Russian literature was being discovered, often via French translations of the originals. The great Scandinavian dramatists Strindberg and Ibsen were to find their works performed on the English stage, both causing minor storms of protest, particularly in the case of such works as Ibsen's *Ghosts*. Certain other European literatures were, however, almost completely neglected in translation, such as that, for example, of the Netherlands and Czechoslovakia, and this state of affairs is only now slowly beginning to be changed by various imaginative publishing projects.

Translation has, however, by no means lost its glamour in recent years. One of the most fascinating episodes during the post-war period was the discovery of the so-called Dead Sea Scrolls. In the early summer of 1947, an Arab shepherd stumbled on a cave near the Dead Sea and brought to light seven ancient scrolls. These were part of the library of a Jewish monastic community in existence before and during the time of Christ. Later, many more scrolls were found, so that they collectively provided an undreamt-of insight into Jewish sectarianism in this very important period. The story of the discovery and deciphering of these Hebrew texts has been related many times in the intervening years and much of it reads as a detective story of the first order. Another post-war episode involving the skill of the translator, archaeologist and linguist has come to be known as the decipherment of Linear B. This involved the deciphering by the British architect Michael Ventris of the script known as "Linear B", and the proof that it was used to record a very early form of Greek. It was one of the great feats of archaeological discovery and upset previous ideas about Greek and Cretan pre-history. It opened up the documents of a civilization older than that of Homer and revealed one of the earliest written languages.

The account of this episode too reads as a painstaking detective story combining a knowledge of a variety of disciplines including that of the linguist-translator.

During the years following upon the end of World War II, the number of translations from and into most languages has grown apace as reference to booksellers' lists will reveal. Several countries now offer firmly established annual prizes for translations, mostly of a literary character. There has also been a marked increase in the translation of scientific and technical literature including, for example, cover-to-cover translations of a number of Russian and Chinese technical journals into English. It is possible for the English reader to purchase numerous first-class, modern translations of most of the world's classics for less than the price of the proverbial packet of cigarettes. The very fact that such translations are published as paperbacks proves that there is more than an adequate market for them. The major works of such authors as Aeschylus, Balzac, Caesar, Chekhov, Dante, Dostoyevsky, Euripedes, Flaubert, Gogol, Homer, Huysmans, Ibsen, Lucretius, Maupassant, Molière, Montaigne, Nietzsche, Plato, Rousseau, Stendhal, Tacitus, Tolstoy, Virgil, Voltaire and Zola can be had in this way, to mention but a few. There are also, on a slightly lesser level, admirable translations of the extremely popular novels by Georges Simenon and Françoise Sagan, all available for a few shillings. The influence of the mass media of the radio, cinema and television cannot be discounted in this general movement in the direction of the popularity of translations. One wonders, for example, how many people might have been prompted by a television series to buy translations of Simenon's *Maigret* stories or by the film to buy the English translation of B. Pasternak's *Dr. Zhivago*. Few people would be puristic or hypocritical enough to consider that this was a bad thing. Likewise, the advent of the paperback within the publishing world has made an enormous impact on the availability of good books at reasonable prices, and translations have inevitably had their share in this.

This chapter could have been presented as merely a bibliography of translations. It has, however, been preferred to indicate some of the general trends and peaks in the translator's art and craft in the hope that these will indicate to readers the part that the former have played in disseminating the world's literature on a wider scale.

READING LIST

Allegro, J.—*The Dead Sea Scrolls—a Reappraisal.* London, 1964.

Chadwick, J.—*The Decipherment of Linear B.* Cambridge 1967.

Dunlop, D. M.—*The Work of Translation at Toledo.* Babel, Vol. VI, No. 2, June 1960, pp. 55-59.

Gordon, C. H.—*Forgotten Scripts.* London, 1968.

Werrie, P.—*L'École des Traducteurs de Tolède.* Babel, Vol. XV, No. 4, pp. 202-212.

CHAPTER III

TRANSLATING AS A PROFESSION IN THE TWENTIETH CENTURY

As has already been hinted at, translating is today a full-time, professional activity for greater numbers of people than in the past, when it was often an activity reserved for the professional writer or the gifted and cultivated amateur. One reason for this has obviously been the vast advances in science and technology coupled with the emergence of many new countries and their gradual industrialization, this also having been accompanied by the setting up of many supranational organizations to control and collate activities in a given sphere throughout the world. Because the translating profession is not yet integrated and controlled to the same extent as, for example, the medical or legal profession, it is difficult to say just how many people are in England engaged in full-time, professional translating, although the number must be in the hundreds rather than the tens or thousands. Professional, full-time translating is thus not as exclusive a profession as conference interpreting or orchestral conducting, but is a very much more exclusive one than accountancy, probably being roughly on a par with that of chartered patent agents, at least in relation to the number of practitioners.

These professional translators, roughly between five hundred and a thousand full-time, are not by any means all engaged in the same kind of translating work, there being various, as it were, vertical and horizontal columns and strata amongst their ranks which we shall be considering in this chapter. Divisions which immediately spring to mind are between translators who are self-employed and those who work for an employer, and between translators who work mainly for information and those who work mainly for publication. Another division, based on subject-matter processed, is between technical, commercial and literary translators. These divisions are, as we shall see, rarely completely distinct, one and the same translator sometimes having a foot in all possible camps.

The easiest method of dealing with the various types of translators is to consider them according to the nature of the material they process. We shall, therefore, base our consideration of the profession on this, dividing our translators into (a) technical and scientific translators; (b) commercial translators; and (c) literary translators, considering various more specialized categories thereafter.

(a) *Technical and scientific translators*

We should begin by stating that this does not mean that the translators are themselves technical and scientific—although they should be—but that the description refers to the type of material they translate. Virtually every subject has today developed to the level of a science or has a technology of its own, be it the making of plastics, the designing of motor car engines or techniques of painting. Hence, translators working in this sphere are engaged in translating material relating to specialized matter in almost every field of learning. There are, however, periodical shifts in the main spheres of science and technology from the translator's point of view, and it could be said that there is probably a fairly reasonable correlation between the spheres in which patent applications are filed in any one year and the major technical and scientific subject-matters requiring the translator's attention in that year. Reference to the annual report by the Comptroller of the Patent Office will show just how the emphasis shifts from year to year. Thus, there will in recent years have been a marked increase in the demand for translations relating to computerized techniques and telecommunications, possibly at the cost of those concerned with the manufacture of new plastic materials and synthetic fibres. In other words, new technologies develop, others decrease in importance, while others continue at much the same level over the years.

Technical and scientific translating, in common with most other categories, can be carried out on a full- or part-time basis. In the former case, the translator will either be working on his own account, i.e. on a free-lance basis, or will be employed by some firm or organization. In the latter case, he will probably be a free-lance or what is sometimes called an "occasional" translator.

Several of the large industrial firms in Britain employ one or more full-time translators, as do various government departments and research organizations. There are, however, relatively few bodies which employ more than five full-time translators, and those employing more than ten can be counted almost on the fingers of one hand. Although internal arrangements obviously differ from firm to firm, there are certain fairly common features in this type of work, so that we can take as our example that of a translator working for an industrial firm.

If the firm is of medium size only, it is quite likely that the translator will work on his own and not as a member of a team or group of translators. He will thus, theoretically at least, be expected to translate anything and everything that comes into the firm in a foreign language. If there has not previously been a translator in the firm, he will possibly have to educate his employer to a certain extent. After all, there are about fifteen to twenty quite important languages used as vehicles of communication in the scientific world, and few translators can really master more than about half of them satisfactorily, even within their own specialized subject sphere(s). The translator will also have to resist requests to translate out of his mother tongue, although most non-linguists find this reluctance very strange at first. After all, the translator is supposed and expected to know "languages"!

The department to which a technical translator will be attached will depend on the internal organization of the firm. It may well be the information service or section, the library or the research department, or possibly also the central services department, since the translator does, after all, provide a service in the sense that what he does could, if necessary, be done outside the firm and also in that what he does contributes to the smooth running and operation of most of the other departments in the firm.

The translator's work will probably fall into three main categories, i.e. letters, material concerned with patents, and articles from technical journals. Let us now consider each of these categories in some detail.

Firstly, and most important as regards urgency, the translator will have to process the various letters coming into the firm in foreign languages. These he will normally have to translate as soon as he receives them, since it is unlikely that any action can be taken on them until they are available in English. These letters will range from enquiries about the firm's products, through those referring to arrangements for overseas visits or complaints, to requests from children for publicity literature, possibly in connexion with a school project. Between these extremes there will be innumerable other shorter or longer letters relating to a wide variety of subjects. To letters, there must also be added, to an ever increasing extent, telexes, since many firms now use this rapid and relatively cheap means of communication in preference to telephone calls which can be much more expensive and often slower too! Telexes from foreign countries often bristle with misprints and, because they are normally in full capitals, it is not possible to indicate

accents and diacritical signs. Hence the deciphering of
them can often offer difficulties out of proportion to their
length.

The translator will find that firms in some countries
always tend to write in their own language, this very often
being the case with the French, for example. Firms in
Germany sometimes write in German and sometimes in
English, while those in the Netherlands write, almost without exception in English, assuming—quite wrongly—that
no-one outside their own country knows or understands
their language. Some firms, for example, those in Italy,
will send both the original Italian and a translation into
English, the latter possibly having been made in their
English office. This is perhaps the best solution to the
problem of correspondence from foreign countries, since
one has an authoritative and correct original text in addition
to a translation into the native language of the country to
which the letter is being sent. Even if it is a luxury, it is a
useful one. Firms in countries having so-called minority
languages, for example, Turkey, Hungary or Yugoslavia,
may well use English or one of the other major European
languages, such as French or German, in their letters,
although this may not always be of the best or most modern
variety. In general, there is much to be said for receiving
a letter, say, in good Turkish or Hungarian, rather than
one in poor, possibly unintelligible German or French!
This, of course, also applies to telexes. The inhabitants of
many foreign countries look upon it as being polite to
write in the customer's language, but this polite gesture
is often misplaced, particularly if the writer is not proficient
in the language. Incidentally, translators can often type the
translations of short letters on the bottom of the original,
this resulting in virtually immediate service (assuming they
can type themselves).

Next in importance after letters in the work of many
translators employed by industrial firms will very likely be

documents of one type or another relating to the prosecution of patents. Patents are both an insurance policy for the firm filing them and a valuable source of information about the activities of other firms throughout the world working in the same field, and most large firms have a patents department which deals with obtaining, prosecuting and possibly also licensing patents as well as remaining conversant with their competitors' patent property. Translations involving patents cover such things as official actions, i.e. letters from patent offices in foreign countries drawing attention to a variety of possible shortcomings in the patent applications filed there by the English firm. There will also, from time to time, be foreign patents cited against an English firm's applications, as well as the checking of translations made in a foreign country of the patent applications filed there. Time is a fairly important factor in most patent work, since dates for filing applications and for replying to official actions have to be complied with. The translator will thus have to give priority to such translations, once he has dealt with the letters and telexes referred to above. The pattern has changed quite considerably over the past few years in relation to the languages which are most important from what we might call patent intelligence work, that is to say patents regarded as sources of information. Up till a few years ago, Belgium was the foreign country which laid patents open to public inspection at the earliest date after filing, this being in the form of photostat copies of the originals as filed. Her place in Europe has now been taken very largely by the Netherlands and West Germany, so that translators now find that they are translating far more Dutch patent applications and German so-called *Offenlegungsschriften* (i.e. German patent applications as filed) and *Auslegeschriften* (i.e. German patent applications as accepted and laid open to public inspection for potential opposition prior to being granted) than Belgian patents as early sources of information on competitors' activities.

French also accounts for quite a lot of patent translations in the information field, in that France publishes a weekly *Bulletin Officiel*, giving illustrated abstracts of recently accepted French patents. Belgian patents can, of course, be filed in either French or Flemish (Dutch), since Belgium is a bilingual country.

During the past ten years or so, many patent abstracting services have also come into being in England and elsewhere, so that abstracts or summaries of new foreign patents or patent applications can be obtained in English on a subscription basis. This means that there has been a resultant shift in linguistic emphasis in patent translation work in industry. It nevertheless remains an important part of most industrial translators' work in one form or another, particularly if litigation takes place in some foreign country involving one of the firm's patents. Needless to say, the abstracting services referred to above have also provided much work for many translators, most of whom work on a part-time, free-lance basis from this point of view.

Brief reference has already been made in Chapter I to trade marks to be filed in foreign countries. These, as another form of industrial property, also contribute to the translator's work in that he is sometimes likely to be asked to check the linguistic and social acceptability of a potential trade mark in various overseas countries. This requires a good knowledge of the language of the country in question as well as of the way in which the possible trade mark can or will be pronounced in that country. It is when such matters as this are considered that the excellence of trade marks such as "Kodak" and "Coca-Cola" or of devices such as the "Wool Mark" is realized when compared with those which have letters or syllables unlikely to be found in certain languages. By contrast, a word such as "Whethy" would have strictly limited possibilities in some countries.

After letters and documents relating to patents and trade marks, the translator will probably find that the bulk of the remainder of his work will be accounted for by articles from technical journals, these also being an important source of information for industrial firms. Each branch of trade or industry has its specialized literature in a variety of languages and this must be searched regularly for items of potential interest to the firm. In some cases, merely a summary of an article or selected parts of it will be required while, in others, a full translation to be given wide circulation will be warranted. Often it will not be the translator who prepares the summary or abstract of such articles, but an abstractor or information officer, the translator being called upon merely if it is a question of a full translation. Although information contained in articles can also be required quickly, it is not normally tied to dates to the same extent as letters or patents, so that this aspect of the translator's work generally has to take third place. Sometimes, the translator will be asked to translate orally sections of an article to the person potentially interested in it. This often obviates the need for a full translation, to the satisfaction both of the translator and his customer, assuming the translator can read the language in question fairly fluently. Incidentally, the translator working on the staff of an industrial firm normally has the advantage, not always shared by the free-lance or the translator working for an agency or bureau, of direct access to his customers. This means that he can consult the customer about difficult terms or concepts or can actually see, let us say, a new machine or process in operation. This is a distinct advantage in many spheres of modern, fast developing technology, in addition to which five minutes spent with a lucid expert can achieve much in helping a translator to understand a tricky point in relation to the workings of a machine or process. In some firms, the translator has, as it were, a peripatetic role, in that he visits the offices of his customers in order to read them translations. In such cases, it often assists him if he can have the material prior to his visit in order to check on the meaning of troublesome expressions, etc.

Returning to journals, many of these, particularly those from Russia and, to a lesser but increasing extent, China, are now published in what are called "cover-to-cover" translations, that is to say the whole contents of the journal is translated into English, although normally with a delay of some months after the appearance of the foreign original. Several of these cover-to-cover versions are prepared in England, while others come from America. Many are produced by professional bodies, others by commercial publishers, in some cases with government financial assistance. If there is no great hurry for a translation of a given article, the translator can sometimes rely on these cover-to-cover translations. Certain foreign and British journals are also now publishing summaries in various languages of their contents (not always in the best or most accurate of forms), while certain others periodically publish full translations in English of the most important articles, usually at quarterly intervals. This practice, too, is often a means of saving the translator unnecessary work, since the last thing he will want is to translate again what someone else has already done, is about to do or is in the process of doing. He will, therefore, always check to see whether a translation already exists or is likely to exist. We shall be considering registers and lists of existing translations in Chapter VI.

Letters, patents and articles are, therefore, the likely three major items of the translator's work if he is employed in a full-time capacity by an industrial firm. This by no means concludes the list, however, since there are many other things he will be called upon to translate from time to time. It is, in fact, precisely because he does not know what he will receive next that makes his work so interesting and varied. He has the potential variables of language and subject-matter to contend with all the time, and seldom is one day's work the same as the last. The translator's work may seem dull and boring to those who know little if anything about it, but it certainly is not to the translator himself. For example, I recently had the following items to deal with in one morning: a chemical test method to be translated from German; a report of an appeal in relation to a patent application to be translated from German; the deciphering of the classification system used in a Norwegian textile directory; a question about the spelling of the name of a German city; a paper in Russian to be sent to an outside translator; the checking of the priority date on a Norwegian patent; the oral translating of a passage of German over the telephone; a letter in French to be translated into English. Quite a varied morning's work!

Some of the other things a translator working in industry might well be required to translate include: so-called status reports on overseas firms with which it is intended to do business or to which credit is possibly to be granted; annual reports of foreign competitors (although most large overseas firms eventually produce these in English too); newspaper cuttings about other firms or their products, possibly as presented or shown at fairs or exhibitions; instructions for the use of a piece of equipment or washing instructions for garments bought abroad; foreign standards; reports of visits made by technical personnel to plants in foreign countries; reports on accidents to members of staff when abroad; references of foreign nationals who are to be employed in England, etc. etc. He will also sometimes be asked to check the proofs of publicity material to be used in connexion with overseas exhibitions or whether the text of an advertisement to be inserted in the foreign press says what it is intended to. He may well, from time to time, have to check the script of a short publicity or television film. He will also, no doubt, be asked to translate a number of private items for other members of staff, for example, letters about holiday accommodation, pen-friend letters (usually in atrocious handwriting and semi-literate in style!), labels on gramophone records, instructions for the use of gadgets bought abroad, etc. He will also be asked by secretaries to decipher the address of a foreign firm from a letter-head or to indicate the telephone number. He is also likely at times to have to take foreign telephone calls or make them on behalf of others, tell someone how to say "good morning" in Czech or "good bye" in Spanish. Thus it will be seen that variety is the very spice of life of the translator working for an industrial firm, particularly if he is operating as a unit. Should he also speak some of the languages he translates from (and everyone will automatically assume that he will), he will sometimes be asked to act as an interpreter, entertain foreign visitors (often to ease the task of those knowing English only who do not relish the thought of having to cope with a visitor knowing little English all day and part of the evening as well!) or possibly merely to sit in at business discussions with foreigners to pick up their asides in their native language. It may also well be that the translator will be required to do a certain amount of teaching of foreign languages to other members of staff, sit on local education committees concerned with the use of modern languages in industry, give the occasional talk on his work to groups of other translators or write about it for professional journals. In the midst of all this, he should also endeavour to keep up with the latest developments in his special spheres of subject-matter interest by reading the relevant English and foreign-language journals. If he has any time to spare, he might well decide to learn another language to add to his repertoire. It is also important that the translator working in industry should be able to absorb the principles and terminology of new disciplines. In the field of synthetic fibres, for example, new outlets are constantly being found and developed, particularly in the direction of industrial uses. Thus, a translator working in this sphere will find that he has to learn to cope with texts dealing with conveyor belts and car tyres, while certain of these fibres are also now being used increasingly in the synthetic leather sphere. Likewise, computerized techniques are now invading most branches of industry, so that the translator will be expected to have more than a nodding acquaintance of them and their terminology. The importance of visits to plants and exhibitions is very important for this aspect of the translator's education.

Although the translator working in industry is a specialist in his own sphere, i.e. that of languages, his work is such that he is unlikely to form part of the general corpus of employees that will be considered for promotion to managerial levels. To this extent, he is restricted in his possibilities of advancement. Nevertheless, he can be an extremely valuable member of the staff of his firm and can, in some cases, advance to the level of what we might call a linguistic consultant, i.e. a person who, although basically a translator, is also called upon to give advice on all linguistic matters arising in the activities of a large firm. In this way, he can increase his usefulness to his employer and, at the same time, contribute to his own advancement.

All that we have said so far in this section applies if there is merely one translator working on the staff of a firm, research organization or government department. In many cases, there will be more than one, one large firm in London having no fewer than twenty translators, although this is the exception, one or two being the average. Often, if there is more than one translator, there will be the possibility for a division of labour or specialization in the direction of languages and subject-matter, if appropriate. In some large translation departments, all its members will be working in one large office, possibly using "silent" typewriters. Although there are obvious disadvantages in this, it does have the advantage that all the translators can, as it were, pool their knowledge and consult one another easily and quickly about their linguistic problems. This arrangement also has the advantage that there need be one centralized reference collection only for the department.

Few translators or translation departments can hope to be able to handle all the material they receive. Surplus or excess material to be translated from common languages or material in languages not handled by the translator(s), as well as material to be translated into foreign languages will normally be sent either to free-lance translators or to translation bureaux or agencies. We shall be dealing with these later in the chapter. If possible, it is, however, always preferable to carry out all translations inside the firm. It is usually quicker, the result is more accurate and cheaper, added to which the information involved is kept within the firm. This does not imply that translators do not have a code of ethics in common with their other professional colleagues, but there is still the feeling among certain clients that translators are liable to pass on information that reaches them in the course of their work. This is, however, not the case, and the members of at least one professional body of translators are obliged to sign and abide by an appropriate code of ethics covering this and other points.

As hinted at, translators will possibly sometimes be called upon to interpret and, if this is occasionally only, most of them welcome the change it offers them from their work in an office although, as was pointed out in Chapter I, translating and interpreting are two very different linguistic skills and activities, seldom combined to the same degree of competence in one and the same practitioner. If the translator is called upon to interpret, he will probably find it better to use the so-called simultaneous method. This means that the interpreter begins his interpretation as soon as the speaker has spoken a sentence or part of it, rather than waiting until the end of what might turn out to be a statement lasting five minutes or more. The original and the interpretation are, as it were, running in parallel, merely being a sentence or so out of phase. The method is also quicker than consecutive interpreting which implies that the interpreter waits until a speaker has said all he wishes to say on any one occasion, only then giving his version of it. Translators should in general, however, recommend that professional interpreters be employed for any important negotiations or visits, since it is foolish and wasteful to attempt to perform a task for one which one is neither trained nor has the requisite temperamental qualities. Most translators resent others trying to do their work and they should ideally adopt the same attitude towards doing the work of interpreters.

How will the translator working in industry get his translation down on paper? Although we shall be dealing in greater detail with this subject in Chapter VI, it may be as well to refer to it briefly here. The method will vary considerably from firm to firm and from translator to translator. It is impossible and unwise to suggest that one and the same method will suit all translators. After all, rules have been said to be for the obedience of fools and for the guidance of wise men, and this dictum applies here too. The following methods may be used and they apply in fact in principle to all types of translators. The translator may write his translation out in long hand, type it himself, dictate it to a typist (either to be taken down in shorthand or to be typed straight on to her machine), dictate it into a machine, or use any combination of these methods, depending on such things as the difficulty of the text, the degree of urgency and how well he knows the language in question. Many translators find it a distinct advantage to type their translations themselves, either as drafts or as final products, since they can, as it were, in this way become self-contained, independent units. It can also be much quicker, since it eliminates the typist's time and also ob- viates checking her work. It should also be pointed out in this context that most of the work carried out by the translator working for an industrial firm will be required for information only and very rarely for publication. Hence, speed with accuracy is more important that stylistic polish. This does not mean that style and niceties of expression can be neglected entirely, but it does mean that much of this work is ephemeral; in other words, once it is read, it has served its main purpose and, providing the meaning is quite clear and accurate, everyone is pleased and fully satisfied. This naturally also affects the way in which much such work will be reproduced. There are, as we have said, many cases in which the translation of a short letter can be typed at the bottom of the original, while there will be others—an important article, for example—in which several copies have to be produced, possibly including photographs, drawings and graphs, intended for wide circulation, in some cases outside the firm. A committee set up by the British Standards Institution is in fact working at present on a standardized method for the presentation of translations.

There are also many other small points that translators have to decide upon in presenting their translations. These include methods of recording and numbering them, as well as of reproducing them. Some of these matters will be considered in Chapters V and VI.

The above remarks on presentation do not imply that translations prepared for information within firms should be slovenly in appearance (although they sometimes are!), but merely that speed and accuracy take precedence over fine presentation. The distinction is one rather of quantity translated and not its quality. After all, if you merely want a recording of a Beethoven Symphony, it would be foolish to choose the most expensive and lavishly presented.

Certain firms and organizations have translations prepared in their final form on tape. In some cases this method is quicker and it eliminates typing entirely. On the other hand, it presupposes that the reader will also have the original in order to refer to tables and graphs, that he will have a tape recorder of a suitable type on which to play the tape, added to which there is always the danger that the recording will be lost or damaged through improper use. Similarly, it is much more difficult to find a specific passage on a tape than it is in a typed translation. The method nevertheless remains as a possibility for those who are attracted to it.

Although it is difficult to set down a standard or accurate figure, most translators working on information work in industry will find that they are translating something of the order of 2,500 to 3,500 words in a day of seven hours or so, although this figure can almost be doubled on easy rush jobs and almost halved in the case of difficult texts on an unfamiliar subject or in a language not handled very often. After all, many words can be translated in the time which it takes to look up one word in a dictionary or check on some point in a reference book. It is also worth mentioning that articles and full translations of patents are often easier and more interesting to translate than short extracts therefrom, since one is, as it were, led gradually into the subject-matter rather than being plunged directly into the middle of it. The quality of the copies from which the translator has to work is also an important factor in his speed on some occasions, this being something not always fully appreciated by his clients. This becomes highly important in the case of such languages as Japanese and Chinese, where very slight differences can make all the difference between one character and another. There is in fact something to be said for providing the translator either with the original document rather than a photocopy or with a magnified copy of it. Good lighting and a quiet office can also contribute positively to the translator's output and the quality of his work. Even such pieces of equipment as revolving bookshelves can ease the translator's work as can desks provided with pull-out flaps. After all, the translator is a specialist, and it is inefficient not to use him as such.

(b) *Commercial translators*

These are quite often classified as a separate category of translators although, strictly speaking, the distinction between it and the previous category is one of subject-matter rather than of basic nature or principle. Commercial translating covers, as the name implies, the translating of what we might call commercial material and general correspondence. Translators working for banks, importing and exporting firms, insurance companies, shipping lines, airlines and travel agencies fall into this category. Their work is perhaps more stereotyped and lacks the greater variety and scope of that of the technical and scientific translator, although it is by no means less important. For this category of translating, a knowledge of commercial principles and practice, finance, banking, economics, tariffs and customs regulations, insurance procedures and the like is important as a background, taking the place, let us say, of a knowledge of medicine or electronics on the part of the technical translator.

Certain translation bureaux or agencies also frequently employ full-time translators in their offices to deal with work of this type from or into the commoner languages, so that they can offer a virtual return service for this kind of material which is normally required quickly.

Relatively few English firms employ so-called foreign correspondence clerks and, if they do, they will usually be found to be nationals of the countries with which they are dealing, as should ideally be the case for a variety of reasons. Such clerks are, however, to be found in many continental countries where the principle of "every man his own translator" also quite often applies or, even worse, of "every typist her boss's translator"! In other words, the Swiss and Dutch, for example, are expected to be able to carry out their own correspondence in the major European languages. Similarly, translators in some continental countries do not, in general, wisely adhere to the "mother-tongue" or "language-of-habitual-use" principle advocated in Chapter I. It must be admitted that many continentals quite frankly over-estimate their written or spoken command of certain foreign languages, no more of them being truly bilingual than people living in England, perhaps fewer in fact, because England has always been *par excellence* a second home for people from a variety of other countries. A little knowledge is no less a dangerous thing in the linguistic field than elsewhere, and it is preferable to under-estimate rather than over-estimate one's abilities. It may be less serious in translating than in surgery, but the principle remains the same. As we said earlier, better a letter in good Hungarian than one in poor German or French. It is consequently better to send your foreign customers a letter in English rather than in their native tongue, unless you have proper facilities for doing so.

(c) *Literary translators*

This term is used to describe translators of all types of fiction and covers such categories as novels, plays, poetry, film scripts and the like, as well as, in many cases, biographies, travel books and similar basically non-technical types of non-fiction. This type of translating differs, in general, from that of technical, scientific and commercial material in that style and mode of expression are far more important than is the case with purely factual material. There is also the point that most such work is ultimately intended for publication rather than merely for information. The responsibility of the translator working in the literary sphere is thus in many ways greater than that of the technical translator in that the former is serving as the agent through whom new works of art in the literary sphere are passed through the language or cultural barrier. This is perhaps also one of the reasons why certain of the great literary works of the past, for example, Goethe's *Faust* or Dante's *Divine Comedy*, have been translated into English (and other languages) several times, whereas no-one would, at least wittingly, translate a scientific or technical work more than once.

Literary translation work thus calls for different qualities or emphases from technical translation work and, usually, there is a fairly clear distinction between both categories of translator. Relatively few literary translators also handle technical work and vice versa, although there is often much technical material tucked away in some works of fiction. Think, for example, of some of Zola's novels or those of Thomas Mann and likewise of a Spanish novel set, let us say, in bull-fighting circles. Most literary translators work on a free-lance basis for publishers and, as we have said, their work is solely for publication. The world of literary translating is also a far more difficult one in which to make a respectable living from full-time translating, and is an activity which tends to be coupled with some other related work, such as writing, teaching or lecturing. Translations of a literary character are paid for either in the form of a fee for the translation—usually at a rate considerably lower than that for technical work—or in the form of royalties, i.e. a percentage of the price of the book for every copy sold. The former method is obviously preferable if the book is unlikely to become a best-seller whereas, if it is or if it is likely to maintain its popularity for a number of years, a royalty basis is the better system of payment. In this sphere of translating, the most lucrative commission is perhaps the translating of a popular foreign novelist's work, such as that of Georges Simenon, on a royalty basis. The translating of children's books can also pay well in relation to the amount of work involved but, on the whole, the literary translator is unlikely to earn as much from translating the same number of words as his scientific, technical or commercial colleague. After all, assuming you know your subject, and unless you do you should not be working in it, the translating of a patent for a new method for the preparation of nitric acid is much easier than a description of a sunset or of the thoughts aroused in someone's mind upon hearing of the death of a loved one. Even the translation of an electronic specification for "Concorde" could hardly be compared in difficulty with a page or two from James Joyce's *Ulysses*, let alone his *Finnegan's Wake*!

Aspiring literary translators sometimes prepare translations "on spec", as it were, and then try to interest publishers in them. This is, however, a very risky undertaking and not one to be recommended, since most translations of books are arranged directly between literary agents and publishers, based ultimately on a reader's report and commercial considerations, and not between translators and publishers. Even a superficial consideration of the economics of publishing will in any case reveal that the publication of a translation is always likely to be a more expensive venture than that of an original work. The translator has to be paid and also the original author and/or his publisher, added to which there will be the reader's fee and ultimately the chance that the translated book will not appeal to the English-reading public. It must also be remembered that translations often have to be edited prior to publication because of shortcomings of a linguistic or subject-matter nature on the part of the translator. Consequently, the publishing of a translation is not something that the average publisher will consider lightly. Some of these difficulties are partly mitigated in the case of certain art books for which the original blocks can be used for the illustrations in the translated version as well. More and more publishing of this type is being carried out today, the same book appearing virtually simultaneously in a number of different languages. On the whole, however, it might be said that translations are fairly common amongst "remainders", and this is not a fate that the average publisher, writer or translator would wish for the fruits of his labours.

The field of literary translating is also one in which contacts and reputation possibly play a greater part than in technical translating. It is also one in which it is often a distinct advantage to know a language which is somewhat off the beaten track rather than, let us say, merely French and German. After all, the awarding of the Nobel Prize for literature to some previously little known author in a country such as Russia, Yugoslavia or India can create a sudden demand for suitable translators to convert his prize-winning and other works into a variety of languages.

A welcome sign of the added recognition being acquired by translators of literary works has been the fairly recent awarding of a series of annual prizes for such translations. Such prizes are now to be found in a number of countries, including England and the Netherlands. We shall be having more to say about them later. This innovation has no doubt also done something to raise the standard of many literary translations, since it must be remembered that most readers of translations are often not in a position, any more than are critics, to judge the original, so that they can, for example, quite wrongly or unjustifiably praise or condemn a translation through their ignorance of the quality of the original. Translators, too, can sometimes commit terrible crimes when translating literature, such as the application of the principle "when in doubt, leave out" or the complete distortion of meanings. Certain linguistic journals are now publishing from time to time quite ruthless criticisms of published translations of literary and other works, and this practice, coupled with various other influences, will do much to improve their general quality. As in most other fields, however, it is both the producer of goods and the purchaser of them that need to be educated.

Many of the best translators of literary works have made it their life's work to translate the works of virtually one author or group of authors into their mother tongue. One thinks here perhaps of Edwin and Willa Muir who were responsible for translating Franz Kakfa's works into English, or of Constance Garnett and, more recently, of David Magarshack who translated many works by such Russian authors as Dostoyevsky, Gogol and others into English. On the poetic plane, one thinks, for example, of Charles Baudelaire who translated many of E. A. Poe's stories and poems into French. A high degree of empathy or, to use the more expressive German term, *Einfühlung*, must be regarded more or less as a *conditio sine qua non* for the successful translating of literary works. Most of us are quite unaware of the amount of pleasure and instruction we have in our lives derived from the labours of literary translators, be they working in the field of fiction, plays or verse. It is, therefore, unfortunate that these translators who were, after all, earlier on the scene than technical and scientific translators should have been overtaken by the latter, at least in relation to the financial rewards of their labours, even if those labours have in many cases been those of love.

(d) *Conference translators*

A seemingly vast number of international and supra-national organizations has sprung up all over the world since the end of World War II, the names of which help to fill our dictionaries of acronyms. Much translation work has arisen as a result of their activities and deliberations. It must also be remembered that by no means all of these organizations are of a predominantly political character. They can deal with anything from iron and steel, coal, air-craft production, health, agriculture, religion and education to criminology, as well as many other subjects of a special-ized character. There is, as a result, a fairly large, but select number of translators employed, either on a full- or part-time basis, by these organizations, and their work consists in preparing translations of the large number of reports, speeches and other documents produced as well as summaries or précis of them. Some translators are also often employed as revisers, let us say, of all the documents relating to a given conference or meeting, ensuring that there is uniformity of nomenclature, style and the like. Most of these people are employed outside England at the headquarters of the various organizations, in such cities as New York (United Nations), Strasbourg (Council of Europe), Rome (Food and Agriculture Organization), Brussels (Common Market or European Economic Community), Paris (United Nations Educational, Scientific and Cultural Organization) and Geneva (World Health Organization). Each of these organizations has its official and working languages, and it is from and into these that conference translators work. It is, therefore, by no means always the case that English will be one of these languages. It is not, for example, for the Common Market, but it is for the United Nations. This means that there can be limited opportunities in these organizations for those of English mother tongue or for those not having a broad knowledge of the relevant working language of a given organization. This fact is frequently overlooked by those hoping to become translators in this field.

The conditions of employment for full-time translators working with many international organizations are roughly comparable with those of the best paid translators working for industrial firms in England, although their salaries and various other fringe benefits, including liability to income tax, can often be far more liberal. This is a field which often appeals to people who are particularly interested in the workings of large organizations of this type and who enjoy working in a multilingual or international atmosphere and who wish to practise their profession abroad, either on a full- or part-time basis, in the frequently rather hectic atmosphere prevailing, in many cases involving a combination of periods of very intensive work, alleviated by the opportunity to relax in comparative luxury between assignments. It is, however, not a field for beginners, but for the mature and responsible translator who can work with a minimum of supervision and checking of his work although, as we have mentioned, revisers are normally used. Conference translators have their own professional association, the headquarters of which are, appropriately enough, in Geneva, the former home of the League of Nations which ended its activities in 1946 when the United Nations was founded.

(e) *Free-lance translators*

This is a term used to describe those who are self-employed on a full-time, but sometimes also on a part-time basis as translators. Such translators normally work from their own homes or offices and carry out translation work for a wide variety of clients. Many full-time, free-lance translators work almost exclusively on material which is to be published, such as books, advertising copy, prestige literature and technical manuals, rather than on purely information translations. Many of them have previously been staff translators who prefer the added independence and flexibility offered by being self-employed. On the other hand, they do not have the security enjoyed by most staff translators, their overheads and expenses likewise being very much higher. For instance, they have to furnish, heat and light an office, accumulate and keep up to date an extensive collection of dictionaries and other suitable reference works, possibly employ a typist, perhaps invest in a photocopying machine, visit their clients or telephone them frequently. Equally well, they do not find their work provided for them as do staff translators, but have to obtain it through their own efforts or reputations. They also have to cope with such things as bad debts, as well as making their own provision for illness and retirement. The amounts earned by free-lance translators are very much dependent on how hard they work as well as on the languages and subject-matter(s) they handle and whether they work for publication or information. For example, a commercial translator working solely from French into English might well have to carry out about three or four times as much work in order to earn as much as a technical translator working from English into Russian in the sphere of publicity literature. Nevertheless, in spite of the obvious hazards involved, few free-lance translators go bankrupt or would willingly return to their former posts as staff translators. It is only fair to add that many staff translators also act in a free-lance capacity in their spare time, in this way usefully adding to their incomes and increasing their experience. Many find that is it a useful corrective to carry out the occasional publication translation in their spare time, particularly if most of their normal work is in the information sphere. Likewise, many other professional people, such as chemists, mathematicians and doctors sometimes work as occasional free-lance translators, particularly if they know an unusual language. Many people who know unusual languages, such as Japanese and, to a lesser but increasing extent, Chinese and certain East European languages, are in great demand as free-lance translators. They cannot, however, afford to specialize so much in relation to subject-matter as those translating from the commoner languages, because of their scarcity value. There are, after all, in England hundreds of people knowing French and German to every one who knows Japanese or Chinese to a comparable level. We shall be having more to say later about ways in which this position can be or is being improved. Finally, many free-lance translators also work for translation bureaux or agencies.

(f) *Certified translators*

This rather unfortunate term does not imply that the translators in question have been segregated from their fellow practitioners, but is used to describe a category of translators found in certain continental countries, such as Germany and the Netherlands, although not, as yet, in Britain. Certified translators are those the quality of whose work has been approved to the extent that it can be accepted in cases in which certified or authenticated translations are required. Such translations are frequently required in legal proceedings, for example, in patent oppositions and the like. Certified translations are also frequently required of such documents as birth or marriage certificates, for example, in applications for naturalization. Certain bodies, for example, the Patent Office, will in England now accept as being "true and correct" translations prepared by certain members of the Institute of Linguists without there being the need to have such translations sworn as being such before a Notary Public, as used formerly to be the case. This latter method has still to be used by other translators. The whole system becomes slightly suspect when it is considered that each and every translation made by any translator should be a "true and correct" one of the original document. In other words, perfection cannot be obtained by legislation.

(g) *Other activities involving translating*

Apart from translating proper, there are a few other activities which involve at least mental translating or a knowledge of the nature and problems of translating, so that they should be included here for the sake of completeness.

We have already referred briefly to the role of the *reviser* in connexion with the preparation of the integrated and co-ordinated proceedings of conferences, mainly on the international level. This activity involves checking material which has been translated before it is circulated or published in final form. In addition to international conferences, it is also sometimes required by publishers prior to the appearance of a book which has been translated, possibly by someone whose knowledge of the language has been greater than his knowledge of the subject-matter or vice versa. This is a state of affairs that arises quite often in the case of the translating of technical books, particularly from rarer languages. Statements such as ". . . translation revised (or edited) by . . ." will be seen more and more today in connexion with technical books translated from such languages as Russian and other East European languages. In such cases, it is virtually essential that the reviser should have before him not only the translation, but also the original from which it was prepared, and it is highly desirable, if not essential, that he should also have a good knowledge of the source language, at least within the subject-matter field concerned. In the case of a poor translation, possibly made by someone translating out of his mother tongue, revision can frequently be a more time-consuming task than translation!

As we have said, revisers of conference proceedings are, more often than not, translators of many years' standing who have, as it were, graduated or been promoted to the office of reviser. This type of work requires a sound knowledge of the source and target languages as well as of the subject-matter in question. It is an activity requiring extreme concentration, a good memory and the ability to acquire an overall picture of a series of texts in order to ensure that there is consistency in the final product. It is, of course, work that can be carried out on a full- or part-time basis.

Abstracting involves passive translating. The abstractor is most likely to be found working in a large firm or in a research organization. The work involves preparing abstracts or summaries in English of articles and other material in various foreign languages devoted to specialized subjects. Abstracting is a very necessary activity today, bearing in mind that so much is being published in every field and language that it is impossible for any one individual, and particularly for one who is, for example, actively engaged in research or development work, to read or evaluate it all. Thus, abstractors act as filters or sieves who hold back the information they know to be new and of interest to people engaged in specific projects.

Somewhat akin to abstracting is *searching*. Searches, for example, of the patent literature in a given very specific field are often required by inventors or patent officers. This again involves sifting through the relevant classes of patents and applications in various languages in order to establish, for example, whether a process which has been developed is novel or that it does not infringe any existing and valid patents. This, too, is work that is often carried out on a part-time or occasional basis.

Dictionary-makers or *lexicographers*, too, should if possible have a knowledge of the theory and practice of translating, since the products of their endeavours are one of the essential tools of trade of the translator, and the more the lexicographer knows of translating the more useful he can make his dictionary. Such relatively simple features as the indication of genders, the indication of the subject-matter field in which a word has a given meaning and the clear indication of various orthographical matters are important in the making and production of dictionaries. They are, however, often liable to be overlooked by lexicographers and publishers who seem unaware of the practical working conditions of the translator. Many dictionaries and glossaries have in fact been prepared by translators as a result of the accumulation of their knowledge of a given specialized field in various languages in the course of their work over

C

the years. It should also not be forgotten that translators are often responsible for introducing new terms into languages, since it is very often they who are first confronted with the need to do so, for example, when finding a word in a language to express a hitherto unknown concept. This need will obviously arise most frequently in the lesser known languages in technical or scientific fields. It should also not be forgotten that words find their way into dictionaries after they have been in use for quite a considerable time. Certain language journals now publish lists of new terms or operate an enquiry service in relation to them.

Brief reference was made in Chapter I to *monitoring*. This activity, practised in relation to foreign-language radio broadcasts, represents in many ways a compromise between translating and interpreting. It involves an understanding of the spoken word, often under very poor conditions, and its reconstitution, as it were, in the form of the written word. The BBC monitoring service at Caversham, near Reading, employs a number of monitors who listen to foreign broadcasts from European, African and Middle Eastern countries and transcribe selected items of news and other broadcasts. It will be remembered that some of these monitors appeared on television during the Russian occupation of Czechoslovakia in August 1968.

Although there is no suggestion that *proof-readers* should be translators as well, it is highly desirable that those handling foreign-language material should have a full knowledge of the orthographical peculiarities of the languages with which they are dealing. Few things can mar an otherwise fine example of printing than omitted accents, words incorrectly split or any one of the other annoying errors that can creep into a text that has been inadequately or inexpertly proof-read. While on this subject, it may be as well to mention that *printers* dealing with foreign-language material and multilingual versions of one and the same document should acquaint themselves with the changes in length of a given text which are likely to result from its translation from or into a given language. For example, it will always be found that a given text translated from Dutch into English and German will result in a longer German text than English text. Such a point can frequently make or mar the setting out or planning of a booklet, particularly if illustrations are involved.

Finally, there is a constantly increasing number of people engaged in *teaching* translating in the many courses that are now available in various countries for training translators, about which we shall be saying more in Chapter IX. This activity is fairly new in England, so that it requires not only teaching and training, but also the production of teaching material with a very specific capability in mind, i.e. the ability to read or translate from a foreign language within a given subject-matter field, without any pretence at an ability to speak or write the languages concerned. It is highly important that those teaching potential translators should be aware of what those translators will be required to do once they are working for an employer or on their own account. The last thing that is wanted in this field is an unwarranted gap between theory and practice, and there are certain dangers that this could arise.

We now come to consider certain other matters which are an inseparable part of the translation scene in the latter half of the twentieth century. These refer mainly to translation bureaux or agencies and to organizations for translators.

(h) *Translation bureaux or agencies*

These are organizations which provide a variety of linguistic services, such as translating, interpreting, typing in foreign languages, printing and proof-reading, as well as sometimes facilities for teaching foreign languages, particularly to business men. Most of these agencies, of which there are now getting on for a hundred in the Greater London area alone, as well as increasing numbers in other parts of the country, send the major part of the translation work they receive to free-lance translators who are specialists, both technically and linguistically. Their clients range from small firms or individuals who occasionally require translations to large firms which send them their surplus material, to be translated into foreign languages or from the rarer languages into English. Some agencies employ a small number of full-time translators in their office to deal with ordinary commercial letters and the like, for which a return service is desirable. Agencies form a useful source of income for many free-lance translators, since the volume of work passing through their hands can be very large. All agencies charge the translator what might be described as commission or a service fee, this being deducted from the fee paid by the client to the agency. Normally, the translator receives between two-thirds and one-half of the fee paid by the client to the agency, the remainder—the commission—covering the agency's administrative costs, possible checking and retyping, advertising, bad debts, etc. On balance, the translator working for an agency will very likely receive less than he would if he were working directly for the agency's client. On the other hand, he does not have to find the work himself. When working directly for a client he is normally likely to be paid his fee within a month of delivering his translation, whereas the agency may well have to wait much longer to receive it from the client. It is, therefore, very necessary that agencies should not be under-capitalized, as some of the smaller ones undoubtedly are.

Very many translation agencies have sprung up in the last few years, as have travel agents, both to meet the obviously increasing demands for the services they provide. In common with travel agents, not all are reputable or reliable, nor as yet do they have a professional association, as do travel agents, which can set and maintain standards, thus offering some safeguard to the often innocent public. The worst agencies act merely as post offices and have not the facilities for checking work or for sending it to suitable translators. Others, however, provide a useful service, both to their clients and to the translators who work for them. One of their main potential advantages is that they can have a very large panel of expert translators—in some cases several hundred scattered throughout the world—on whom they can call depending on the subject-matter, source and target language involved. Some also handle the production of publicity literature from the translation stage right through to the printing stage, thus saving small firms not having any experience in this field much trouble and expense. It must however, be stated quite definitely that only reputable agencies, that have a reputation to lose rather than the unlikelihood of ever establishing one, should be used, since bad translations are always too expensive and can cause havoc to your own reputation. It is also worth remembering that few agencies will accept responsibility for errors in their work and losses to their clients resulting from them. It is, therefore, definitely a case of *caveat emptor*, even in these days when there is so much legislation to protect the customer from his own follies. It should perhaps also be mentioned that certain Chambers of Commerce provide translations for their members as do some professional bodies, in this respect functioning as translating agencies.

(i) *Organizations catering for the interests of translators*

Having now described the various categories of translators and the kind of work they perform, it will be appropriate to conclude this chapter by considering the major organizations of a national and international character that cater for the interests of translators as members of a profession. As we have said in Chapter I, it is highly desirable that all translators should belong to such professional organizations. There are many reasons for this, not the least of which is the opportunity it affords them to meet their professional colleagues and discuss questions of common interest and concern with them. The fact that translators are not, as yet, organized to the same extent as members of the legal or medical professions, for example, means that they are unlikely to improve their position to the desired extent unless they act as a corporate group, and it is the various organizations that we shall now be considering which offer them that opportunity.

(i) *The Translators' Guild.* This body, founded in 1955, is under the auspices of the Institute of Linguists, itself founded as long ago as 1910. The Institute itself is an association of linguists as a profession, organized on the lines of other professional bodies. Its members include lecturers and teachers, technical, scientific, commercial and literary translators, interpreters, librarians and information scientists, as well as linguists occupying positions in commerce, industry, administration, the Civil Service, the Armed Forces and other professions. The Institute publishes a quarterly journal, "The Incorporated Linguist", which contains articles of interest to linguists working in all spheres. The Institute has an extensive collection of dictionaries and glossaries together with reference grammars and books for private study at all levels, together with various language courses on gramophone records. It also arranges conferences on topics involving the collaboration of linguists with those in other professions and occupations. The Institute also holds examinations in late May and early December in a wide variety of modern languages and at various levels, the highest two of which—Final and Intermediate—lead to qualified membership. At the highest level there is a translator and interpreter option in addition to the more general examination. The Institute also awards annual bursaries for practical linguistic research projects.

Membership of the Translators' Guild is open to those Fellows and Members of the Institute who work as translators and who have satisfied the Guild committee of their competence in various languages and subject-matters. The names of the members of the Guild are listed in the Translators' Index published by the Institute. The present membership of the Guild is in the region of 250. Most of its members are working in various specialized technical fields rather than in the literary sphere. The Guild periodically holds meetings of its members at which matters of interest are discussed. It also publishes a Newsletter for its members, which contains a section on terminology problems. Through the Council of the Institute, the Guild also sets down minimum translating fees for its members, these being applied fairly generally throughout the profession. Members of the Guild also subscribe to a code of Professional Conduct which deals with such matters as fees, advertising and encroaching. It also has powers to institute disciplinary action in cases of gross professional misconduct on the part of its members. It also maintains contact with various overseas professional bodies for translators.

(ii) *The Translators' Association*. This is a group within the Society of Authors, which was established in 1958 for the purpose of concerning itself exclusively with the interests of translators into English. The general previous lack of such a body, particularly in the literary sphere, had been responsible for the fact that translators had increasingly become the least respected and least rewarded members of the literary community. The Association felt bound, in the first instance, to concern itself more particularly with the problems of translators of books. The scope of the Association's activities has now been extended to cover translation in every form and medium, although the majority of its few hundred members is still literary rather than technical or scientific translators. Membership of the

Association is normally confined to translators who have had some form of translated work published or produced in the United Kingdom. Although practically all languages are covered by members, the largest representation is for French, German and Italian. It is interesting to note that the Association has largely been responsible for arranging awards for the best translations of books produced in the United Kingdom from certain languages. These include the Scott-Moncrieff Prize for translations of French twentieth-century works of literary merit and general interest, the Schlegel-Tieck Prize for German twentieth-century works of a similar character, and two John Florio prizes, one for translations of Italian works published prior to 1900, the other for translations of similar works published in the twentieth century. The translated books must be submitted by the publisher and not by the translator. The awards normally range from £200 to £400. The Translator's Association does not have its own publication, but matters affecting translators are dealt with from time to time in *The Author*, the journal of the parent Society of Authors.

(iii) *The Aslib Technical Translation Group*. This is one of the many specialized groups in Aslib (Association of Special Libraries and Information Bureaux), the leading organization of its type within the British Commonwealth and having members throughout the world. The Group membership is composed, for the most part, of technical translators, information scientists and librarians employed by British industry or operating on a free-lance basis. Regular meetings of the Group are held at which there are lectures or discussions on a wide range of subjects of special interest to the translators and others for whom the Group caters. There are also occasional Group visits to industrial translating sections and the like. The Group also issues a Bulletin three times a year, circulation of which is restricted to members of Aslib, containing the texts of many of the lectures given at Group meetings. It also contains a list of new dictionaries and glossaries, as well as having a terminology section giving the meanings of new terms in a variety of languages.

In addition to the Technical Translation Group, Aslib, the parent body, also operates a register of specialized translators, mainly in technical fields, as well as handling the Commonwealth Index of Unpublished Translations, to which we shall be referring in Chapter VI. Papers of interest to translators are also, from time to time, published in the *Aslib Proceedings*. Matters of interest to translators are also frequently featured in the many courses put on by the Education Department of Aslib. One of these referred to the nature and use of foreign-language dictionaries. Aslib has also published certain works of interest to translators, including a Guide to foreign-language printed patents and applications.

(iv) *International P.E.N.* This world association of writers was founded in 1921 by C. A. Dawson-Scott and now has a membership of about 8,000 in its eighty or so Centres throughout the world. Its general secretary operates from the office of the English Centre in London. The initials P.E.N. stand for Poets, Playwrights, Editors, Essayists, Novelists, but membership is, in most countries, also open to all writers of standing, including translators, in which field the various P.E.N. Centres have some outstanding members. The International P.E.N. holds conferences, some of which have been concerned largely with translating, such as that held in Rome in 1961, devoted to "Translation and Translators". The published report on this conference contains much of interest to translators, not only of fiction, but also of verse, plays and film scripts.

(v) *Fédération Internationale des Traducteurs* (F.I.T.). This is a body, under the auspices of U.N.E.S.C.O., with its headquarters in Paris, which was founded in 1953 with the purpose of federating the various national societies and organizations for translators throughout the world, with the aim of improving their position and status. F.I.T. holds congresses periodically in different European cities at which matters of interest to translators in the widest sense are discussed. It also has a number of sub-committees concerned with special aspects of translating, such as literary translators, international bibliography of translation, prizes for translation, technical and scientific translators, terminology and documentation, training and qualifications of translators, translation of legal documents, history of translation, and copyright. Most of the national societies of translators in various parts of the world are affiliated to or are members of F.I.T., although there is no United Kingdom member at present. F.I.T. has for a number of years published a quarterly journal, appropriately entitled *Babel*, which contains articles of interest to translators of all types, as well as reviews of new dictionaries and a list of mono-, bi- and polylingual glossaries and articles on translation that have appeared in other journals. From time to time, special issues of *Babel* have dealt with such subjects as the translation of sacred texts, the machine translation of languages, translation in Africa, translation in Asia, and the cinema and translation. The proceedings of two of the F.I.T. conferences, namely the third, held at Bad Godesberg in 1959, and the fourth, held at Dubrovnik in 1963, have been published, respectively as *Quality in Translation* and *Ten Years of Translation*.

Several of the European member societies of F.I.T. publish their own journals, for example, those in Belgium, Denmark and the Netherlands, the society in the latter country also publishing a periodic list of its members after the style of the Translators' Index of the Institute of Linguists.

It is also worth mentioning that U.N.E.S.C.O. itself publishes an *Index Translationum*, being an international bibliography of translations. Volume 20, which appeared in 1969, contained a list of 39,450 translations published in 74 countries during 1967. This will give readers some idea of the volume of translations being produced at the present time.

(vi) *Association Internationale des Traducteurs de Conférence* (A.I.T.C.). This body, which was founded in Geneva in 1962, has as its object the study of problems arising from the exercise of the profession, to defend the moral and material interests of those who practise it and to maintain high professional standards. The membership of the Association is composed of revisers, translators and editors and it has about 200 members. It issues a yearbook and a quarterly bulletin, together with various other documents of interest to its members, including a model letter of engagement. It has since it was founded succeeded in negotiating improvements in rates for its members. Readers may be interested to know that these, in common with those of the Association Internationale des Interprètes de Conférence (A.I.I.C.), are normally quoted in U.S. dollars and are *per diem* or daily rates for free-lance practitioners.

READING LIST

Adenis, J.—*The Conference Translator*, The Incorporated Linguist, October 1968, pp. 83-86.

Adkinson, B. W.—*The Role of Translation in the Dissemination of Scientific Information*. Babel, Vol. IX, No. 4, 1963, pp. 176-181.

Brawley, J.—*The Technical Translator in Industry and Problems surrounding his Profession*. Babel, Vol. XV, No. 4, 1969, pp. 213-215.

Burns, M.—*The Work of the Translator*. The Incorporated Linguist, July, 1963, pp. 70-77.

Burrows, H. Sefton.—*Translation at United Nations Headquarters*. The Incorporated Linguist, April 1963, pp. 45-48.

Clifton, P. A.—*International Advertising*. Aslib Technical Translation Bulletin, Vol. 13, No. 2, Summer 1967, pp. 50-62.

Gingold, K.—*Translation in American Industry*. Babel, Vol. X, No. 3, 1964, pp. 114-117.

Readett, A. G.—*The Organization and Work of the National Coal Board Translation Section*. Babel, Vol. IV, No. 3, September 1958, pp. 160-165.

Veillet-Lavallée, F.—*La Traduction dans une Organisation Internationale*, Babel, Vol. VIII, No. 4, 1962, pp. 188-193.

CHAPTER IV

SPECIAL CATEGORIES OF TRANSLATING

It could no doubt be said that every category of translating is a special category. There are, however, certain spheres of translating work which, for one reason or another, demand a special faculty or combination of skills, such that we are justified in considering them separately from the types already dealt with. These special categories involve the translating of the Bible, the translating of verse and vocal texts and, finally, the translation of film scripts. These we shall now consider briefly in turn.

(a) *Translating the Bible*

Surprising as it may seem, the Bible is still the world's best-seller followed, I am led to believe, by the thoughts of Chairman Mao Tse-tung and the works of Dr. Spock—an interesting result, no doubt proving an excellent subject for future psychological interpretation! The translation of the Hebrew of the Old Testament and the Greek of the New Testament is an activity which has engaged the minds and skill of translators in most countries for the past several hundred years. Equally well, it is a task which is still going on and one that shows every sign of continuing for many years to come. There is even a special journal, "The Bible Translator", devoted to this category of translating.

It will, consequently, be possible here to give merely the briefest outline of the subject, referring to a few special landmarks and indicating the magnitude of the activity.

The translation of the Bible has in fact the oldest and most continuous tradition of any type of translating in the western world. Its origin extends back to the second century B.C., when the Old Testament was translated from Hebrew into Greek for the benefit of the large Greek-speaking Jewish community in Egypt. This translating of the Bible has continued to the extent that complete Bibles are now available in well over 200 different languages, while parts of the Bible have been translated into more than 1150 languages and dialects throughout the world! This makes the twenty or so languages into which certain other books have been translated seem insignificant. Unlike many other types of translations, the translation of the Bible into a given language is not a task which is carried out once and for all, but is one that is subject to more or less continuous revision, often involving completely new translations. Reasons for this are new evidence on the original texts, new views in relation to interpretation, changes in the languages into which the translations are being made, and new ideas as to what constitutes adequate communication. It has, in fact, fairly recently been suggested that no translation of the Bible should be allowed to remain unrevised for more than twenty years and that no version should be left unrevised for more than fifty years. Although the translating of the Bible is a highly specialized sphere, involving linguistic, theological and palaeographical skills, it is nevertheless one from which all translators can learn much. The account, for example, of the methods employed for the preparation of the New Testament section of the New English Bible, which appeared on 14th March, 1961, and of the Old Testament and Apocrypha in March 1970, makes fascinating reading in any context. Equally well, the publicity given to the event and the vehemence of the reactions to the new translation served to prove more than amply that the Bible is still definitely "news" in the sphere of translating as well as in purely religious circles. The result was a fine tribute to English scholarship. It is also important to realize that the Bible can be read at various levels or in different contexts. In addition to being the religious book of countless people, it also contains the account of certain historical events and, read in this way, constitutes a general historical text. It has also contributed many quotations which have become part of our general linguistic usage. It is also often suggested that reading of foreign-language versions of parts of the Bible, one of the Gospels, for example, can be a useful aid in learning to acquire a reading knowledge of those languages. It is assumed here that the subject-matter will be relatively familiar, so that attention can be focused on vocabulary and constructions. The only disadvantages in this method are that certain foreign-language versions of the Bible still make use of archaic words and constructions and also that much of the vocabulary is in any case likely to be divorced from everyday matters and concepts. The Bible can, however, be a useful aid in this direction, if wisely used.

It is also important to realize that the translation of the Bible or parts thereof into a given language has often played a significant part in codifying that language or in assisting to confer upon it a recognized, standard form. This claim is usually made, for the most part justifiably, for the translation of the Bible into High German made by Martin Luther, the New Testament appearing in 1522, while the complete Bible became available in 1534 with Luther's translation of the Old Testament. Luther's translation of the Bible met with much praise and much criticism when the first part of his translation appeared. To meet this criticism, he set out the principles he had applied in a very instructive document entitled *Sendbrief vom Dolmetschen* in 1530, a work that is still worth reading by all translators. He advocated in it the importance of writing not a Latinized German, but a native idiom.

Luther's Bible was for many years the Bible of the

Germans, as were the respective versions prepared at the time of the Reformation in several other languages, it frequently being many years before more modern versions were made more in accordance with modern linguistic usage. After all, languages have changed considerably in the 400 years or so since many of these classical translations were prepared.

We have already referred briefly in Chapter II to the part played by missionaries in preparing translations of parts of the Bible into obscure languages or dialects, some of which had previously not existed in written form. This was necessary in order to provide the people, for example, in remoter parts of Africa, Asia and America with the word of God in their own tongues. Although most missionaries were far from being trained linguists or translators, many of them have done sterling work in this field, and it is to them that we owe the first written accounts of some languages and dialects. One of the best Japanese-English dictionaries has, for example, been prepared by someone who was for many years a missionary in the Far East. Consequently, translation may justifiably be regarded as a major fringe benefit of the activities of missionaries which could, from other points of view, sometimes be questioned.

Another minor impetus to the translation of religious and liturgical texts into various vernaculars was the abolition a few years ago of the sole use of Latin in various Roman Catholic services. There are many who regret this step, in that the universal use of Latin, for example, in the Mass provided a great unifying element in the Church, whereas there has been a linguistic barrier between most other churches since the Reformation. There is, therefore, much to be said for the use of a supranational language in religious services. There are also those who consider that this would be advisable for certain scientific communications, but it is unlikely that this will ever become a generally accepted or practised view. After all, we have only to think of our reluctance to accept a few minor improvements in the text of a Psalm or possibly of our aversion to hearing a hymn which formed part of our daily fare at school sung to a different tune. Also, it is not only in the religious sphere that emotional considerations cannot be divorced from translations. We are all prone on occasions to confuse the messenger with the message or the medium of the message with the message itself.

(b) *The translating of verse*

The translating of poetry or verse must surely be a case *par excellence* in which the old Italian saying *traduttori, traditori* (translators—traitors) applies. Few things are more difficult than the effective and true translating of poetry into poetry (if, indeed, it is at all possible), although it is an activity that never ceases to arouse the imagination of translators, possibly because of the challenge it inevitably offers.

Even if we consider words alone, they have at least three qualities, namely sense, sound and emotional quality, only the first of which is normally separable from the whole and can find a suitable equivalent in another language. Further elements in a poem are metre, rhyme and probably a greater use of figures of speech than in prose. To expect to be able to transfer these as well in a translation, without loss, even in the case of a ballad, which is perhaps the most "factual" and unemotionally laden poetic genre, is a task fraught with virtually insuperable difficulties and, of course, one offering a corresponding challenge to the translator, becoming all the greater the more one approaches the realms of symbolist poetry with its added element of private and esoteric worlds.

Each person, translator or not, has to find his or her own private solution to the question of the translating of poetry. To some, the best solution has perhaps been found in the

series entitled *The Penguin Poets*, the purpose of which, to
quote from the general editor's foreword, is "to make a
fair selection of the world's finest poetry available to readers
who could not, but for the translations at the foot of each
page, approach it without dictionaries and a slow plodding
line by line." These "translations" are in fact prose translations which give the reader at least the sense of the original.
He can then refer back to the original as and when required
by the extent or lack of his linguistic knowledge. The series
now contains volumes devoted to French, German, Italian,
Spanish and Russian verse, together with a few volumes
devoted to individual poets, such as Baudelaire, Rimbaud,
Pushkin, Novalis, Hölderlin and Lorca. Although each
volume usually has a different translator, the same principle
as outlined above has been preserved for each. It could be
said that such a presentation is suitable only for people
with at least a modicum of knowledge of the original. It
is, however, such that it could well arouse a desire to acquire
this and has, no doubt, in many cases done so. After all,
people are encouraged or inspired to learn languages for
even more curious reasons.

There are, when considering the question of the translation of verse, two very apt quotations from the works of the
Dutch poet, Willem Kloos (1859-1938). In his study of the
Dutch poet, Jacques Perk (1859-1881), Kloos wrote: *Vorm
en inhoud bij poëzie zijn één, in zooverre iedere verandering in
de woorden een gelijkloopende wijziging geeft in het beeld of
de gedachte, en iedere wijziging in deze een overéénkomstige
nuanceering van de stemming aanduidt.* (Form and content
are one in poetry in that every change in the words produces
a parallel modification in the image or thought, and every
modification in the latter denotes a corresponding nuance
of the mood.) The other statement by Kloos which is
relevant here is that *kunst is de aller-individueelste expressie
van de aller-individueelste emotie* (Art is the most highly
individual expression of the most highly individual emo-

tion). Incidentally, should readers knowing Dutch think that the proof-reader has nodded in relation to these quotations, I should hasten to point out that they are in an "old" form of Dutch spelling!

The first of these quotations implies that a poem represents a delicate balance of highly sensitive elements, the changing of any one of which will inevitably upset that balance. An analogy from the sphere of music would seem to suggest that one cannot, for example, play a Bach Prelude and Fugue on the modern pianoforte, unless one is prepared to obtain a result different from that when the same work is played on a harpsichord or clavichord. This is, of course, true, although it could be argued that the form and content have not changed, although the content has, in fact, in relation to timbre and, in one case, to method of sound production, i.e. plucking in the harpsichord rather than striking in the pianoforte and clavichord. Kloos' second statement defines art as being something very personal and unique in the best sense of the word. This again suggests that any attempt at translation must inevitably result at least in an adaptation or transposition. One wonders, incidentally, what Kloos thought of the translations into German of certain of his sonnets made by Stefan George or into English by Th. Weevers and others. On a lower level, it suggests the proverbial attempt to place a square peg in a round hole. Art and poetry, which is merely one facet of art, thus emerge as highly refined and distilled expressions of personal experiences, images, feelings or thoughts, these expressions having resulted from a continual process of refinement and polishing. They result from a desire to realize the thought expressed in a poem by the Chinese poet, Mong-Kao-Jen (eighth century), being one of the collection translated into German by Hans Bethge and used, in slightly modified form, by Gustav Mahler for the first section of the last movement of *Das Lied von der Erde*. It reads, in Bethge's translation, *Ich sehne mich, o Freund, an deiner Seite die Schönheit dieses Abends zu genießen* (I long, o friend, to savour the beauty of this evening at thy side), surely being a feeling most of us have experienced at one time or another and one that must lie at the very essence of the true artist's endeavours. This whole process of writing poetry results in an almost epigrammatic concentration of emotion and feeling, so that we might also regard poetry as expressing the commonest feelings and emotions—in the sense that they are part of the common experience of human beings—in the most beautiful and succinct manner. Compared with poetry, prose must appear as utilitarian, as in fact the prose translations of "The Penguin Poets" are.

Descriptions of the nature of poetry and even of the would-be translator's task in relation to it are legion and could well form a substantial chapter in any collection of quotations. Unfortunately, for the most part, they merely describe the position, without being able to offer any really useful or adequate suggestions for its solution. Nevertheless, this does not deter translators from attempting what most must realize is an impossible task. It could be that they are thinking of a quotation from Goethe's *Faust*, i.e. *Den lieb' ich, der Unmögliches begehrt* (I love the person who desires the impossible). There is, however, always satisfaction in attempting the impossible, and it has sometimes proved successful, even if not always in the sphere of translating verse into verse. An interesting point on which to reflect in this context is the experience of some of the mediaeval mystical poets and writers who found that even their own mother tongue proved inadequate for the expression of the feelings and emotions they had in relation to their Creator!

It may seem as if I have implied that the task of translating verse into verse is, as it were, doomed to failure from the start and should, therefore not even be attempted. Although this is, perhaps, my personal view, I think it is possibly one of a linguist who, let it be admitted, has greater direct access to the originals of world literature, be they in poetry or prose, than other people. It is for the same reason that linguists are sometimes unwilling to visit a foreign country unless they have studied its language beforehand, feeling they will, as it were, be linguistic *personae non gratae*. We shall, however, look at various attempts to translate one poem when we come to consider translating in practice in Chapter V.

(c) *The translating of vocal texts*

A vocal composition, be it a Lied, chanson, opera, oratorio, cantata or even a potential candidate for ephemeral fame in the "top ten", may be likened to an intimate union of a musical and vocal line into which enters a large number of sensitively adjustable variables, the altering of any one of which will, inevitably, put the whole out of balance. Having said this, let us consider some of the ways in which the translator endeavours to overcome the seemingly impossible task involved in converting, let us say, *Die Zauberflöte* (German original) into *The Magic Flute* (English), *Il Flauto Magico* (Italian), *De Toverfluit* (Dutch), *La Flûte Enchantée* (French), *A Varázsfuvola* (Hungarian) or *Volshebnaya Fleita* (Russian).

Bearing in mind the difficulties we have outlined in the previous section in relation to the translating of verse which is, after all, the standard form of expression in most vocal texts, apart from recitative, we have in vocal music to match the new text to the original melodic line, with its characteristic rhythm, pitch, harmony, timbre and many other subtle factors which may enter into the union of words and music. When we consider, for example, the intimate way in which J. S. Bach wedded his texts to the melodic line, accompaniment and/or obbligato instruments, making use of the typically baroque "musical symbolism"

discussed at great length by Pirro and Schweitzer, we encounter an added difficulty facing the translator of such
vocal texts. Equally, if we read the correspondence and
discussions between Richard Strauss and Hugo van
Hofmannsthal concerning the libretti of such operas as
Der Rosenkavalier, we learn of the scrupulous attention
often given by librettist and composer to the successful
marriage of words and music. A further point to be borne
in mind is that the original texts of many operas and songs
have often been lamentable from the literary point of view
—illustrating, incidentally, interesting aberrations in the
way of literary taste on the part of certain composers—
and have thus been saved from justified oblivion merely
by having been set by composers of genius. This applies
both to several of Schubert's songs and to certain of J. S.
Bach's cantata texts, which have no claim to immortality
when they are divorced from their musical settings, as well
as to the major proportion of the so-called lyrics of the
average pop song, the impact of which is about as long as
that of the sound of a cork on being withdrawn from a
bottle!

We gain an interesting insight into the methods of at
least one gifted nineteenth-century translator of opera
libretti into German from the account given by the critic,
Eduard Hanslick, in *Fünf Jahre Musik* of Max Kalbeck's
method for translating the Czech libretto of Smetana's
Prodaná Nevěsta into German as *Die Verkaufte Braut* (The
Bartered Bride). Kalbeck did not know a word of Czech,
but had the literal German translation written under the
original Czech for him. As a poet, he brought the contents
into German verse and, as an experienced musician, he put
the correct word under the correct note. It sounds so
simple! We thus see perhaps that the translator of vocal
texts should be both a poet and a musician. After all, it
has been said on more than one occasion that none but a
poet should translate a poet. Although this method seem-

ingly worked quite well in Kalbeck's case, I should feel
it better if the translator knew both the source and the target
language. If this is not the case, it may well be that an adaptation rather than a translation will result. A highly interesting comparison can be made, at a slightly lower musical
and literary level between the original version of a song
popularized by the late Edith Piaf, namely *Milord*, in its
original French version and the Dutch version, sung by
Corry Brokken, and an English version, sung by a male
singer. Comparisons are said to be odious and cannot but
be subjective when the interpretation of musical works is
concerned. This English record also raises the point as to
whether a male should sing a song obviously intended for
a female. The only sin of omission in this context is, to
my knowledge, the failure of a male singer to perform
Schumann's song cycle *Frauenliebe und -Leben*. It is however apparently not a transgression of musical transvesti-
cism that females should sing Mahler's *Lieder eines fahrenden
Gesellen*.

In the words of one critic, "certain English translations
of nineteenth-century operas are characterized by incredible
slovenliness, illiteracy, unsingableness and downright
drivelling ineptitude". This is a serious accusation when
it is borne in mind that the translator is the person largely
responsible for introducing a new vocal work to the public
of a given country. To reach the ears of the audience and
to be understood should be the first objective of any word
spoken or sung on the stage. I say spoken or sung since
there is much spoken dialogue in certain German operas
and in most operettas. Think, for example, of *Fidelio*, *Die
Zauberflöte*, *Die lustige Witwe*, to mention but a few. Likewise, there is much recitative in the Italian operas of
Mozart and in such works as Bach's *St. Matthew Passion*,
this in some ways representing an intermediate stage between
the spoken and sung word. It must also not be forgotten
that words are more difficult to understand when sung than

when spoken, particularly if they are sung to a full orchestral accompaniment, and that this difficulty is increased in the case of female voices. There is a story of the words "Where is my Cressida?" in William Walton's opera *Troilus and Cressida* sounding suspiciously like "Where is my dressing-gown?" in a certain performance. I must personally admit that, although English is my mother tongue, I have much greater difficulty in understanding words sung in English than, let us say, German or Italian. In some cases, I have to listen for quite a while before I realize that a work is in fact being sung in English!

Many of the English translations of operas by Mozart, Rossini and Meyerbeer referred to above tended to use poetic words wherever possible, added to which there was the tendency to introduce inversions in word order, for example: "I will defeat the foe" became "I will the foe defeat" or even "The foe defeat will I". One choice example reads:

> Faithless, I wrought in unknowing falseness,
> Binding by bargains that hid mishap.

It could perhaps be argued, at least in the case of opera, that the scenic or visual element partly compensates for a text, either the original or a translation, which is not fully understood. I feel, however, that this is an unnecessary compromise. It has also been argued that the presentation of operas in the vernacular is one method of encouraging the establishment of a national opera in those countries where this form has not yet perhaps taken its full and right-ful place in musical life, such as possibly in England and the Netherlands. There is said to have been a request from many lovers of opera to have more works sung in English and this is perhaps confirmed by the appearance of new translations of such works as *Rigoletto* and parts of Wagner's *Ring*. Andrew Porter, who has prepared certain of these more recent translations of opera libretti into English, has stated that he has kept three essentials in mind. Firstly, the meaning must be clear and direct. Secondly, the translation must lie naturally on the music, in other words, the verbal phrasing must not contradict the musical phrasing, as is so often the case. Thirdly, the translation must "translate" the original, it must remove obscurities in the original and will thus probably result in a more direct version.

On the other hand, it could also be said that the whole root of the problem of the translation of vocal texts lies with the audience which should be prepared to make itself familiar with the text or libretto either in its original form or through line-by-line literal translations—after the manner of the "Penguin Poets"—or full synopses, but in no case through so-called singing translations which frequently differ considerably in meaning from the original. An example from Puccini's *La Bohème* will suffice to illustrate the point. The Italian original is: *Che gelida manina, se la lasci riscaldar. Cerca che giova? Al buio non si trova. Ma per fortuna—è una notta di luna.* This has become in one English singing translation: "Your tiny hand is frozen, let me warm it into life; our search is useless, in darkness all is hidden. Ere long the light of the moon shall aid us." The sense in the second part of this quotation is not reproduced very accurately in the English translation. The translator cannot be blamed for this, since it is obvious that something must be sacrificed in such a singing translation. Although a translator, or perhaps precisely because I am a translator, I should very much prefer a literal prose translation into English of the libretto of an opera to be sung in a language I did not know. In this context, I can remember a number of years ago hearing a performance of Beethoven's *Fidelio* at Covent Garden in which certain of the singers sang in the original German and others in English! I do not, however, suggest that this is in any way an ideal or appropriate solution.

Concerning the question of the translation of vocal texts

into the vernacular, it is interesting to note that a Dutch translation of the text of Bach's *St. Matthew Passion* was prepared about twelve years ago with the thought that it would be welcomed by the Dutch public. This turned out to be far from the case, the familiar original German text being vastly preferred, in spite of the emotional overtones of German in the Netherlands in the years following the end of World War II. The effect was analogous to that produced by a new translation of, let us say, a familiar psalm or the replacing of Latin by the vernacular in the Mass. This could well be said to apply to most vocal texts that are, by their very nature, firmly embedded in a given cultural or linguistic milieu. There is a possible analogy here to the dubbing of films rather than using sub-titles. There are those who think it incongruous, to say the least, to hear the music of Mozart being sung in English, in the same way as there are those, myself included, who find it difficult to reconcile the fact that German, for example, is proceeding from the lips of Bob Hope or Bing Crosby in, let us say, "The Road to Zanzibar". The lesser evil seems to be the use of sub-titles for the films and for television productions of operas, such as are in fact often used now. It is interesting to note that the principle adopted in "The Penguin Poets" has also been extended to translations of the words of certain well-known *Lieder*, also published by Penguin Books Ltd.

Assuming, however, that translations of vocal works are insisted upon, then the translator thereof must know his source and target language, must understand the difference between what is to be read and what is to be sung and heard, must be an accomplished musician with a practical knowledge of voices and acoustics and of such things as the best vowels and notes in a singer's range and, last, but not least, must also be something of an artist and poet. He must, therefore, as it were, be an orchestrator of words in addition to his other qualities. As one translator of some of Schubert's songs has put it, "As a pastime, I can strongly recommend it. Cross word puzzles and chess problems are, by comparison, very dull and unrewarding." He nevertheless equally admits that "perfection lies far beyond our grasp."

(d) *The translating of film scripts*

With the close of the era of silent films about forty years ago, the world lost yet another form of what might have been regarded as a universal means of communication, recalling the saying of that ancient and respected Chinese philosopher, Confucius, that one picture was worth several thousand words (a sentiment more likely to meet with the approval of an engineer than a first-year student of Chinese or Japanese!). Be this as it may, we are now left virtually only with mathematical equations and chemical formulae as bearers of universal messages or possibly with a musical score which, in addition, is more than likely to use Italian for indications of tempo and the like.

Most early silent films were full of action, so that only the occasional sub-title was required to supplement the visual image and the moods suggested by a pianist accompanying it. With the advent of "talkies" however, the scope of subject-matter for films widened considerably, and the cost involved in producing them also made it at least desirable that they should be shown in countries other than that of their origin. In other words, a means had to be found to transcend the language barrier inevitably associated with the "talkies", since people will not tolerate attending a film in a language they do not know, whereas there is less reluctance to do this in the case of an opera.

Two solutions were found to this problem. One was an extension of the use of sub-titles, such as had been used with extreme parsimoniousness in the case of silent films, while the other was the replacement of the original sound track by a new one in another language, making the original actors appear, as it were, as ventriloquists.

Strangely enough, perhaps, these two methods seem to have found different degrees of favour and acceptance in different countries. Sub-titles are definitely more popular in English-speaking countries, while dubbing, as the second method is called, seems more popular in non-English-speaking countries, particularly in France and Germany. The Netherlands, with the generally excellent knowledge of foreign languages on the part of its inhabitants, again seem to favour sub-titles. In many ways, sub-titles give the best of both worlds, since the original sound track is there for those who can understand it, while the sub-titles provide the rest of the audience with at least an abbreviated account of what is being said on the original sound track. I say abbreviated account, since to include everything would be impossible, bearing in mind that it takes longer to read even one line than it does to speak it. It is in this process of condensation that the difficulty and art of sub-titling lie. The result is often likely to be a sort of telegraphic style which can be either amusing to those who can follow the original or annoying to those who cannot.

The far more challenging, difficult and expensive method is to provide a completely new sound track in another language, the system known as dubbing, which is possibly the strictest of all aspects of the translator's art and craft. Here the difficulties increase enormously, since each utterance in the original has to be matched in the dubbed version by an utterance of equal length and one which coincides, as far as possible, with the lip movements and facial expressions of the original actors and actresses. If this is not the case, then the lack of synchronization is far more disturbing than the inability to understand the original. There is an added factor, which cannot be overcome at all, but which disturbs some people even more, such that they prefer sub-titles in all cases. It is the psychological difficulty referred to in the previous section of hearing, let us say, French proceed from the mouth of a well-known American actor. It is, of course, possible that this disturbs the French far less than the Americans and, after all, the dubbing is being done for the immediate benefit of the French. We experience the difficulty when foreign films are dubbed in English, although this does not occur all that often.

The dubber is immediately faced with a collection of seemingly impossible tasks. Such matters as characteristic differences in word order in different languages have to be taken into account, for example, the placing of an adjective before a noun in English and after it in French, and the habit of the German verb to find its way to the end of a sentence. Likewise, there are great differences in lip movements and sound in English *love*, French *amour* or between English *die* and French *mourir*. Some languages are also much more concise than others, for example, the Hungarian needs but one word to express three English words in such cases as *kertemben* (in my garden) and *szeretlek* (I love you).

Perhaps the best term for the translator engaged in this type of work is dubbing writer. He is in the position of having to realize that his written version will eventually be spoken. It is his task to make phonetically dissimilar dialogue appear visually similar while still preserving the semantic and stylistic parallel between the original and dubbed lines. He must mould the text to make it fit the lip movements on the screen, remembering that many of these will be close-ups. This synchronization of lip movements is more important even than committing the sin of mistranslation. His activity is really allied more closely to the cinema rather than to literature. It may be described as audio-image synchronism or as the marriage of the phonetic beast to literary beauty. Most dubbing writers use their own system of diacritical marks or signs to indicate the shape or position, i.e. the visual aspects, of the lips. Having, as it were, coded the original, the dubbed version must, when coded, coincide as far as possible with that original. The dubbing writer is also faced with other problems, such as whether to retain the foreign flavour of the original with the actors affecting accents and using foreign expressions, or to create the illusion that the script was originally written in the dubbed language. The whole cinema is, after all, an art of illusion, being based on an example of the optical variety, to which there is added in dubbing one of the audio variety. Dubbing writers rarely appear as public figures and often tend to be forgotten amongst the innumerable credits associated with feature films. Their work is however extremely skilled and deserving of much greater appreciation and attention than it usually gets.

Much easier is the task of the dubbing writer if it is a question of an industrial film or a travel film which will very likely have a commentary rather than dialogue. Very many short instructional films are made today by industrial firms in all parts of the world, and the provision of translations of their commentaries is a sphere in which certain translators specialize. The trade in television films and serials is also another sphere in which writers of sub-titles and dubbing writers find themselves involved. Think, for example, of the great success of *The Forsyte Saga* by John Galsworthy, copies of which have been sold to a number of countries, including Russia.

It will thus be seen that the work of translators is by no means static, having to adapt itself to changes and developments in other spheres of communications.

READING LIST

Babel—Vol. VII, No. 2, 1961 (special issue devoted to Bible Translation).

Babel—Vol. VI, No. 3, 1960 (special issue devoted to Cinema and Translation).

Babel—Vol. IX, Nos 1-2, 1963 (special issue devoted to Translation of Sacred Texts).

Cary, E.—*Traduction et Poésie*. Babel, Vol. III, No. 1, March 1957, pp. 11-32.

Ege, F.—*Zur Übersetzung von Gesangstexten*. Babel, Vol. XV, No. 2, 1969, pp. 95-97.

Glenny, M. V.—*Linguists in the Theatre*. The Incorporated Linguist, July 1966, pp. 79-81.

Hamberg, L.—*Some Practical Considerations Concerning Dramatic Translation*. Babel, Vol. XV, No. 2, 1969, pp. 91-94.

Holmes, J. S.—*Forms of Verse Translation and Translation of Verse Form*. Babel, Vol. XV, No. 4, 1969, pp. 195-201.

Levy, J.— *Die Übersetzung von Theaterstücken*. Babel, Vol. IX, No. 2 1968, pp. 77-82, 102.

Mounin, G.—*La Traduction au Théâtre*. Babel, Vol. XIV, No. 1 1968, pp. 7-11.

Mund, A.—*La Traduction Lyrique—Art, Science et Technique*. Babel, Vol. XIV, No. 3 1968, pp. 144-151.

Pocar, E.—*Über die Möglichkeit der dichterischen Übersetzung*. Babel, Vol. VI, No. 2, June 1960, pp. 72-76.

CHAPTER V

TRANSLATING IN PRACTICE

We now come to the most practical chapter in our book. It will be our aim to take the reader into the translator's study or office, as it were, and to observe him at work. Translation is, as we have seen, both a craft and an art and is, as such, partly teachable and partly unteachable, in the same way as it is possible to teach people the principles of musical composition, while it is impossible to teach them to compose on the level of, let us say, Bach or Mozart. It is, however, possible to point out pitfalls, procedures which are more likely to result, other things being equal, in a good rather than a mediocre or poor translation. This chapter consequently contains a number of examples taken from a variety of foreign languages in order to illustrate the problems arising in their translation into English. By its very nature however, it must be regarded as a study in width or breadth rather than in depth, since it would be impossible to consider all the problems likely to occur in translating, let us say, Russian into English in a matter of fifty pages or so.

We shall be considering here both technical and literary texts, but predominantly the former. We have already dealt sufficiently with the various specialized categories of translating in Chapter IV for a work of the present dimensions. It is also more likely that the readers of this book will be interested from the practical point of view in technical or scientific translating rather than in literary translating.

It will in this context be as well to dispel, from the start, a fairly popular misconception. It is that concerning the alleged clear-cut line of demarcation between literary and technical language. A view seems to prevail in some quarters that technical and scientific material is written using elements that are quite different from those employed in everyday and literary language. We cannot, unfortunately perhaps, make the startling discovery, as did M. Jourdain in Molière's *Le Bourgeois Gentilhomme*, namely that he had been speaking prose all his life, in relation to differences between technical and literary language. There are obviously cases in which different languages are used for different purposes such as, for example, the elaborate honorific language used in certain circumstances in Japanese; but broadly speaking we are more likely to find differences between spoken and written language than between various categories of written language. Dutch, for example, has many "written" counterparts to words used in the spoken language.

Words, are of course, the basic units of any text, and the essential building blocks of any text will be the same, usually small words., These are the words that join statements together, i.e. conjunctions, the words that indicate the relationship between objects, i.e. prepositions, and the words that indicate how, when and where things are done, i.e. adverbs. The words which describe things, i.e. adjectives, the words indicating actions, i.e. verbs, and the words giving the names of things, i.e. nouns, on the other hand, depend to a much greater extent on the nature of given text. In other words, they are much more specific, while the former categories of words are far more general. Thus, words such as: catalyst, acid, basic, polymer, fumaric acid and acetaldehyde are likely to be encountered in a chemical text only, while words such as: play, house, garden, car, tea and milk are likely to be found in an average newspaper article or novel. Words such as: ere, homeward, slumber,

D

gait and scintillate are, on the other hand, more likely to be found in a literary or poetic text. It is, therefore, important that any word count in a language should indicate very clearly the sources that have been used for its compilation. The more or less specialized words listed above will however be linked together by the same hard-working, ubiquitous conjunctions and prepositions and it is more than likely that they will be qualified by a general set of adverbs. It is, therefore, the specialized words that differ from text to text, in other words, the trimmings rather than the basic building units. There is also the point that scientific and technical language is intended to be precise and unequivocal in meaning, while more licence can be allowed in personal interpretation in literary and poetic language. Unfortunately, not all scientific writing is by any means clear and precise—this being one of the main sources of difficulties and resultant errors and ambiguities in translations —since many scientists and technologists are notoriously bad at expressing themselves via the written word and sometimes too via the spoken word. The same word can of course, be used in a variety of texts and will possibly then have differing meanings or auras of meaning. For example, the word "winter" in a sonnet will be surrounded by a whole series of overtones, giving it a very colourful timbre, whereas the same word in a meteorological report would be akin to a note produced on a tuning fork, that is to say without the overtones or harmonics which result in a rich timbre. It is as if the average technical report were being played on a series of tuning forks, while a poem is played by a string quartet or wind ensemble. In the same way, the botanist does not see the same tree, at least professionally, as did, let us say, the painter Vincent van Gogh, any more than love will mean the same thing to a psychologist and to a young couple experiencing it, possibly for the first time.

Having therefore established that the differences between

technical and literary language are those of register or timbre rather than of basic nature, we shall now consider how the different criteria of a good translation, as set out in Chapter I, affect the translator in practice.

The first prerequisite for achieving any of these criteria is that the translator should understand the text fully in the source language. This from his point of view involves understanding it to the same extent as would a native-speaker of that source language who was suitably versed in the subject to which it refers. For this, the translator must have a full knowledge of the grammar of the source language, of its basic, non-specialized vocabulary as well as of the vocabulary specific to the subject of the text. He must also have sufficient understanding of the subject matter to enable him to read between the lines of a poorly written original and, as sometimes happens, to enable him to spot errors in the original text, due to the author's ignorance, poor proof-reading or even to the mundane, but highly important matter of a poor copy from which he often will have to work. Too little attention is given to the quality of photocopies given to translators, particularly in such languages as Japanese and Chinese, this being a point involved in what we might call "customer education". In order to be able to do all the things set out above, the translator's knowledge of the source language must be without any gaps and his knowledge of the subject matter must be more than adequate to the task in hand. He will, of course, be permitted various aids in the way of dictionaries and other reference works about which we shall be saying something in Chapter VI. This, then, is the equipment that the translator brings to his text. If he is lacking in this equipment or if it is faulty, then his task will be all the more difficult, if not impossible, and the result of his endeavours will likewise fail to rise beyond the poor or mediocre.

We now come to the criteria by which it will be reasonable to judge the result of the translator's labours. The most important of these will, in all cases, be that it should present an accurate account of the contents of the original, omitting nothing and likewise adding nothing. This implies a complete understanding of the original in every way coupled with a corresponding knowledge of the target language. Such requirements are most likely to be met by a person who has the target language as his mother tongue, language of habitual use or of adoption over a long period and who is, at the same time, conversant with literature on his special subject in that language. A good criterion of this latter point is the ability to hold one's own with experts in that subject who are not linguists. For example, a translator of texts relating to organic chemistry should be able to chat with organic chemists, possibly at a party, without them realizing that he is not an organic chemist. He should, in other words, know the correct jargon and be able to use it correctly and intelligently. He should not, as it were, commit malapropisms. This criterion applies equally well to all other disciplines and specialized spheres in which translators work. This background and subject knowledge is gained over the years by study and reading and is also aided by regularly processing texts in the respective sphere of specialization.

Having understood the text in the source language, the translator must then be able to reconstitute it, as it were, in the target language, using all the facility that he would if he were writing an original document in that language. In other words, his readers must ideally be unaware that they are reading a translation. They must gain the same impression of the text, as a piece of writing, as they would if it had been written by one of their English colleagues, assuming that the translation has been made into English. This is what Tytler meant when he said that the translation must have all the ease of an original composition. This is, of course, a requirement of a translation which can be fulfilled to a very much higher degree by a person who is translating into his or her mother tongue rather than one who is translating out of it, since it will very likely be through a misplaced word or an incorrect tense that the non-native-speaker will betray his lack of intimacy with the target language. Such sentences as "I am already being here since six weeks" are not part of the educated native English-speaker's mode of expression. The other component determining the correct meeting of this criterion is that the translator must know when to refer to a "girder" as opposed to a "beam", when to "water vapour" as opposed to "steam", when to a "thread" as opposed to a "fibre", "filament" or "yarn". There are very few, if any, genuine synonyms, and it is usually such that there is but one really correct word in a given place or context and it is up to the translator to use it.

The third criterion of a good translation is that it should capture the style and atmosphere of the original. This is more important and difficult in the case of literary texts which are very often not contemporary and which, more often than not, are set in a cultural milieu different from that in which the target language is spoken. This criterion does not occupy such an important place in the case of scientific or commercial texts, since most of these will be contemporary and, when all is said and done, a chemical laboratory, a piano factory or an operating theatre are more or less the same the world over. Style and atmosphere are, however, sometimes important in certain commercial letters, for example, those notifying a complaint, and in legal documents, such as licensing agreements and patent specifications. Likewise, there are, to say the least, conventions when, for example, describing experiments used to illustrate some new process or principle.

If the translator has fulfilled all these criteria in the manner we have set out above, then there is a reasonable likelihood that he will have produced a good translation or, at least, one worth being considered as such.

Before moving on to consider in greater detail some of these stages in the production of a good translation, we must revert to the distinction made in Chapter I between information and publication translations in the technical and scientific sphere, since the criteria set out above may be relaxed a little in the case of information translations. The translator in this field must, of course, understand the original grammatically and also basically in relation to its subject-matter, although his knowledge of it need not always be as profound as that of the publication translator. He may, for example, be permitted an occasional "oxygenated water" instead of "hydrogen peroxide" or "fear of heights" instead of "hypsophobia" in a psychological text, but he should not confuse "hydrogen peroxide" with "water" or "hypsophobia" with "agoraphobia". Likewise, his translation may sometimes read as if it were a translation, sometimes even betraying the source language by the use of an awkward construction or the like. Such faults or shortcomings will be overlooked by the reader who merely wants information rather than aesthetic enjoyment or satisfaction. The speed at which most information translators are required to work precludes the production of consistently perfect stylistic and terminological results. The information translator, must however, succeed in making a legal text sound like a legal text and not like a section from a cheap novel and a commercial letter like one and not like a love letter, but excessive attention to style and atmosphere will normally be refinements he can reasonably dispense with. As we have already said, most literary translators work for publication and they must therefore not allow themselves the stylistic licence allowed in many information translations. It will, therefore, be seen that the translator should always be informed whether his translation is for information or for publication.

Let us now assume that a translator has received a text in one of his source languages relating to a subject with which he is conversant and that he is told to prepare a translation of it into his mother tongue since it is desired that the text should be published in an English journal relating to that special subject. How will he set about translating the text? We shall now be setting down certain general recommendations, based on experience, but in common with many other such rules and recommendations, it will often be found that they can or will be broken or disregarded. Yet, as we have implied before, the time to break or disregard them is when this is done intelligently and with a full knowledge and realization of what can be involved. Once again, the saying that rules are for the obedience of fools and for the guidance of wise men applies to a certain extent.

The first golden rule, by no means always observed, is to read the whole of the original text before beginning to translate one word of it. There are several good reasons for this advice. First of all, it will enable you to gain a general impression of the text, its subject-matter, depth, linguistic and subject-matter difficulties, style and the like. Such an initial reading-through often serves to convince a translator that he is thoroughly out of sympathy psychologically with the author, particularly in the case of a literary work and that, therefore, it would be better for all concerned if he were to refuse to translate it. A technical translator can also come to this same conclusion in relation to the subject-matter or language of a given text. After all, there are limits to everyone's knowledge of certain languages and subject-matters, and it is much better to say "no" at the beginning than to be wishing one had said it while carrying out the translation. If a translator feels that he cannot really understand the language or subject-matter well enough without more or less constant reference to a grammar, dictionary or encyclopaedia, then he had better reject the commission. After all, even on an economic level, it is possible to translate several tens of words in the time it takes to look up one word in a dictionary, and time is also money to most translators. Likewise, a translation is likely to be good in proportion to the translator's knowledge of the language, subject-matter and sympathy with the original author's style. There are, let it be admitted, cases in which a translator will, quite successfully, not only not read the whole text before beginning his translation of it, but will even begin putting down his translation of a single sentence before he has read to its end. This is a case of breaking the rules when you know the dangers and pitfalls involved in doing so! It should also be mentioned here that it will often be necessary or advisable to read the whole text of a patent specification or of an article in order to be able to translate the claims of the former or a summary of the latter. The preliminary reading of the full text assists the translator to work himself into the subject and will also enable him in many cases to judge in what sense particular terms are being used.

A further piece of good advice is not to translate the title of an article or book until you have completed the whole translation. This is because titles, particularly of books, are often difficult or impossible to translate literally, and by the time you have translated the whole work, you may well have thought of a much more suitable translated title than you could have before making the translation. Much can be learnt from comparing the original and translated titles of books and films. Very often they bear little resemblance, frequently for very good reasons.

Having assembled the reference works he is likely to need for the translation, this having been assessed from a preliminary reading of the text, the translator will proceed to make a draft translation. Such a step or procedure is virtually essential in the case of all translations intended for publication, since most translators, whether they like to admit it or not, inevitably have second thoughts about the best way in which a given thought or concept can be expressed. Likewise, particularly when translating long works, there is the danger that the translator will not be thoroughly consistent in his terminology, and this can be checked when the draft is being corrected or revised. How the translator prepares his draft will depend very much on his own preferred method of working and on the facilities he has at his disposal. Personally, I prefer to type it myself, thinking better through the written or typed word than the spoken word and preferring typing to writing in long hand. Others may prefer to dictate the draft translation to a typist or to use a dictating machine of some type.

There is much to be said for completing the whole translation in draft, even in the case of a book, before beginning the second and final stage, i.e. that of polishing and correcting the draft into what will emerge as the final version of the translation. Needless to say, the draft should be typed or written with plenty of space between the lines so that any necessary changes can be incorporated. It is then advisable to leave the draft for a few weeks before beginning the polishing stage. This enables the translator to view it with a certain degree of detachment and objectivity whereas, if he begins his polishing immediately after finishing the draft, he will still be too close to the original. Readers may be interested to know that this present book was prepared in the same way. Firstly a draft of the whole was prepared, containing many gaps, the original being prepared a month or two after the completion of the draft, by which time many other points had been thought of which could be included at appropriate places in the final version. Similarly, the reading lists were not compiled until the whole book was completed.

There are also some translators who prefer to prepare their draft without any reference aids, merely using these, as and where necessary, at the polishing stage. It may well also be that the translator will need to consult his client or the original author about obscurities and ambiguities in the original text, and this is often best done once the draft translation has been prepared. If it is not possible to consult the client or the author, this sometimes being the case if the translator is working for an agency that may not disclose the name of its client, then the translator will have to put his remarks in relation to ambiguities and the like in the form of translator's notes. He should not pass over matters he does not find clear without drawing the client's attention to them, nor should he on any account leave out what he does not understand. Likewise, he should not eschew asking his colleagues or others about points which are not clear to him. After all, we cannot be omniscient, and many doubts a translator may have can hardly be held to be shortcomings on his side, since he will not by any means always receive perfect texts to process. Humility too is by no means a bad fault in any translator.

The polished draft will then have to be typed, preferably by an expert or professional typist, since there will have been little point in producing a good translation if it is poorly presented. The excuse, "I'm a translator, not a typist", is hardly likely to enhance any translator's reputation. Translators working for publication must also ensure that their final copy is in every way fit to be presented directly to the printer for setting, bearing in mind that the printer may not be in England and may, therefore, not be dealing with the setting of his mother tongue. Consequently, all ambiguities must be eradicated and any instructions to the setter must be given clearly and in a manner that will be intelligible to him. Before sending his translation to the client, the translator will check it once again for such points as missing lines, words or punctuation, spelling errors, etc., since few typists are perfect. If the text is a mathematical one or includes tables or figures, formulae and the like, these too must be doubly checked, since a misplaced decimal point or zero can make quite a difference in such documents. All conversions of units, etc. must also be checked if they have been carried out by the translator. All corrections must also be made on all the copies of the translation. The translator should also always keep a copy of all translations he prepares, preferably to be filed away with the original text. There is also much to be said for keeping the draft version too, since much can be learnt from comparing it with the final version in months or years to come.

In principle, this procedure will be followed by all translators, with a certain degree of licence and corner-cutting, commensurate with their skill and experience. The same basic procedure should also be followed with information translations, except that the luxury of a draft will very often be dispensed with here, since it is quite possible for experienced technical information translators to prepare their finished product in one stage. In this way, their output can be quite considerable and, on balance, they will probably earn as much as their publication colleagues, since the lower fee normally paid for information work will be compensated for by the greater output compared with the publication translator and his higher fee. The one factor common to both types of work must however be strict adherence to the content of the original. No compromise is permissible here.

We have not said much about the actual process or mechanism of translating. It is in fact very difficult to explain this, in the same way as it is difficult to specify the individual stages involved in the brain when holding a conversation with someone or when reading a book in a foreign language. The point is also of little more than academic interest from the point of view of this consideration of the subject. Suffice it to say that much of the translator's work consists of the operation of a series of conditioned reflexes. One important point can however be made here, and that is that the translator is dealing with the conversion of thoughts from one language to another and not merely of individual words, even if those thoughts are, ultimately, expressed by a series of individual words. To paraphrase Nietzsche, we might say that translating involves an *Umwertung aller Gedanken* or possibly an *Umwertung aller Worte*, but certainly not an *Umwertung aller Wörter*! That is to say, it is a conversion of thoughts, possibly of words in context, but not of individual words. This is a very important point for novices to realize since they often experience great difficulty in getting away from too slavish a following of the original text in relation to such matters as word order and constructions. This does not necessarily mean that a translation should be excessively free, particularly in the case of technical material, but that it should not give the impression that a square peg has, as it were, somehow been forced into a round hole. After all, a language and thoughts in it are living and sensitive entities and both must be treated carefully when being transferred out of their native milieu into another which might be quite different in structure. There is certainly some correlation between at least the form of thoughts and the medium in which they are expressed and this fact cannot but affect the work of the translator. Such factors are, as we shall be seeing, one reason why computers can, at best, hope to be used for the production of crude information translations and never for literary or publication translations. The degree of licence, loosening, reshuffling and regurgitating which can be permitted in relation to the original in its passage to a new language is something concerning which the translator will develop a sort of instinct during the course of his career. He must at all times remain conscious of words and sensitive to their possible meanings and effects on others. Words are not as precise as mathematical or chemical symbols, and the meanings attached to them are often conditioned to a large extent by our own personal environment and attitudes. The translator must, therefore, remain conscious of and sensitive to possible personal auras of meaning in the choice of words.

Having now considered in general the process of translation, we shall go on to look in greater detail at some of the pitfalls and difficulties involved in translating a variety of material from various languages into English, indicating in the process some of the forms of Scylla and Charybdis lurking on the translator's path.

First of all let us consider briefly the main languages from which translations, again predominantly of a technical or scientific nature, tend to be required in Great Britain. Although they naturally vary somewhat from discipline to discipline and although the proportions vary from year to year, as a result of a number of factors, not all of which is predictable, there are certain fairly well established patterns.

There are few branches of science or technology in which German does not still constitute a prime, if not the prime source of information, added to which many classical reference works, particularly in chemistry, are in that language. It must also be remembered that German is not only the language of West and East Germany, Austria and one of the four languages of Switzerland, but that it is also used in certain cases as a means of communication in various Central European countries, mainly Czechoslovakia and Hungary, particularly if they are directing their attention towards the West. Consequently, it will be found that most translators in Great Britain have German in their repertoire and, if they do, it is likely to account for much of their work, irrespective of their field of specialization.

The position of French has, in many respects, receded in the last few decades, and it no longer occupies the same important position it once had, at least in the scientific and technical sphere. It is, however, still one of the important languages from the point of view of translations into English, being used in France, part of Belgium and of Switzerland, as well as being one of the official languages of Canada. It is also somewhat of a *lingua franca* in certain East European countries, particularly Poland and Romania, as well as occupying a similar position in the Middle East and Northern Africa. For historical reasons, most translators educated in Great Britain will have French in their repertoire, although this does not apply to the same extent to those born in other countries.

Russian is today a highly important language in a wide variety of scientific and technological fields, since the Soviet Union now takes her place alongside most other highly industrialized nations and is producing important results in many sophisticated spheres of learning. This is also shown by the fact that a number of Russian journals is now produced in English cover-to-cover translations, both in Great Britain and the United States. Russian is also one of the three possible languages in which senior science graduates can take a so-called reading course. As a result of various waves and campaigns in recent years—not the least of which have been via radio and television— there is now quite a number of translators and research scientists who can handle Russian, so that there is no longer a real shortage of translators from Russian into English. The position in Great Britain is, however, by no means as favourable in the other direction, at least as far as Russian mother-tongue translators with an up-to-date knowledge of modern Russia and resident in Great Britain are concerned.

A language which has made its presence felt in numerous scientific and technical fields in the last two or three decades is Japanese. Japan has long since passed the imitative phase and is now a highly industrialized and advanced country producing important research findings in most fields. In certain spheres, such as the manufacture of certain types of electrical equipment and in ship-building, she virtually leads the world. There is in Great Britain a very definite shortage of competent translators from Japanese into English and those there are can hardly afford to specialize because of their small numbers.

German, French, Russian and Japanese are then the "big four" which are common, to a greater or lesser extent, to most disciplines. After them, the languages of importance depend very much more on the specific discipline considered and also, of course, on the nature of the organization requiring translations. For example, in the sphere of mining, Polish and, to a certain extent, Dutch must be added, since coal mining has been an important industry in these two countries. In the field of paper-making, Swedish becomes important, since that country is a major producer of wood pulp. Although the synthetic fibre industry is now found in most countries of the world, much valuable research in this field is now being carried out in Czechoslovakia, so that Czech and to a lesser extent Slovak are likely to account for a certain amount of the work of translators in this field. Similarly, Italian is quite important in the petrochemical sphere, Spanish in the commercial sphere, because of trade with South and Central America, while Chinese is beginning to make itself felt in various branches of science and industry.

When we come to consider the translation of literary works into English, the importance of various foreign languages presents a different picture. French, German and Italian are probably the main languages from which translations into English are made, although other, often minor languages, such as modern Greek, Hungarian, Dutch and Finnish, can become important, particularly if a previously little known author from the countries concerned is awarded the Nobel prize for literature. Think, for example, of the interest shown in the works of Boris Pasternak when he was offered the Nobel prize a few years ago.

Having considered the major languages in the field of translating, we shall now look at their position and that of certain other languages in the main linguistic families, drawing attention to specific difficulties involved in translating them into English.

The main European languages from the point of view
of translating can be assigned to the following three
families:

1. Germanic languages: English, German, Dutch, Danish,
Swedish, Norwegian and Icelandic;
2. Romance languages: French, Italian, Spanish, Portuguese and Romanian;
3. Slavonic languages: Russian, Polish, Czech and
Slovak.

Languages such as Finnish and Hungarian belong to a
completely different group from the majority of European
languages, i.e. the Finno-Ugric and not the Indo-European
family, showing no real affinities, either in construction or
vocabulary, with the languages in the families listed above.
Japanese too is in a class on its own, as is Chinese. Incidentally, it should be realized that there is no relationship
whatsoever between Japanese and Chinese, except merely
that Japanese is written partly in the same characters as
Chinese. We shall have more to say about the nature of
Japanese later.

Since English is a member of the Germanic group, the
other languages in that group show the greatest affinities
to it, and it is partly for this reason that they are perhaps
easier for English mother-tongue translators than languages
from other groups. German is, of course, very much more
highly inflected than modern English, added to which it
has, comparatively speaking, a very rigid word order which
is really incompatible with its high degree of inflexion.
Latin too was a highly inflected language, but had, by way
of compensation, a very free word order. German sentences
can be very long, with the main verb often tucked away
at what can seem a very remote end. This feature shows
itself particularly in the claims of patent specifications,
which are traditionally in one sentence, such that much
mental juggling has often to be carried out before an ac-

ceptable version is arrived at. The following exaggerated example of a notice shows to what excesses this final positioning of the verb in German can lead: *Bekanntmachung —Der der den der den Pfahl der an dem Weg der zu der Brücke die über den Fluss geht führt steht umgeworfen hat angeben können wird belohnt!* (A reward will be paid to the person who can denounce the person who knocked down the post on the road leading to the bridge!). Another feature of German which seems forbidding to many non-linguists is the large number of very long words. These compounds may, at first sight, seem formidable, but they are in fact usually much easier to decipher than their Romance language counterparts. To use the word *Schreibmaschine* for *typewriter* is much more logical and consistent than to use *machine à écrire*, as do the French. Compound nouns in German (and other Germanic languages) are always such that the last component indicates not only the gender of the noun, but also the category or class to which it belongs, in our case a "machine", while the first part(s) of the compound indicate the modification of that category or class in the given case, in this one a "machine that is used for writing". This profusion of compound nouns in German was parodied by E. F. Bozman in a piece concerned with translating from various European languages. It is, I think, worth quoting. "The from the German into the English language translation by no means a so easy a task as it appears to be is. It is ever important for the translator on the one hand to preserve as far as possible the delicate shades of meaning of the author's thought, the height-depth and the light-darkness of his not only never-decreasing but also ever-increasing ego-personality, and on the other hand to render him into recognizable English while at the same time retaining the characteristic rhythm of the wonderfully variable if perhaps rather sometimes often somewhat over-flexible Germanic idiom. A translation is a union-conjunction through the mind-intellect of two embodied soul-spirits, the author self-revealed through his writing consciousness for the one part and the translator self-submerged while at the same time self-expressed for the other part. By the finished two-product the reader is enabled to explore through a language perhaps known or perhaps unknown to the author the recesses and abscesses of his mind-brain through the spiritual medium of the interpreter-translator. The author and the translator twin-kindred soul-minds together-linked in self-subconscious personality-union must be; so a wonder-fine translation produced is. Naturally!"

Another feature which hardly offers any difficulties in present-day German, but which can frequently be found in pre-war texts and reference books, is the use of Gothic or *Fraktur* type. This can of course be learnt in an hour or so and is far less of a problem than the Russian alphabet or the excessive number of diacritical signs used in, let us say, Hungarian, Czech or Polish. There is also a characteristic German form of handwriting which can offer very real difficulties to those not conversant with it. Translators are quite often required to work from handwritten documents and notes, and it is very important that this should form part of their training. A similar problem arises of course in the case of such languages as Russian, Yiddish and Hebrew.

With a good knowledge of German and an English mother-tongue, it is normally quite possible and usual for a translator to learn to translate from Dutch, Danish, Norwegian, Swedish and Afrikaans, within a given special-ized subject sphere, using what might be called a process of triangulation. There is an interesting article on this process, in relation to Swedish, by E. van Haagen. Icelandic is not, however, a language that can be approached so easily by this method, since it has changed but little since the days of Old Norse and is still as far from modern Nor-wegian as modern English is from the language of Beowulf.

This process of triangulation is one that can be used to a limited extent only in the information sphere. It cannot be applied in the literary and publication spheres, since there is, in the former, likely to be a much greater use of figures of speech and idiomatic expressions, for a successful recognition, identification and translation of which a much deeper knowledge of the source language is required. Those unfamiliar with them may well encounter difficulties in positively identifying Danish, Norwegian or Swedish at first sight. There have been cases of translators setting to work on a Danish text with a Swedish dictionary, it being quite a few words later that they have discovered their error!

As we have implied, although French is likely to be the first foreign language of the majority of people in Great Britain, be they translators or not, it is by no means the easiest from which to translate into English. This also applies to speaking, there being relatively few Englishmen who can speak French really well and vice versa. French grammar is, compared with German or Russian, relatively simple. Its vocabulary is largely derived from Latin and has much in common with that of English, through the Norman conquest, yet it is far less precise than German, partly as a result of the method of forming compounds indicated above and a wide use of small particles. For example, compared with German *was ist das?* French *qu'est-ce que c'est?* seems a far more complicated way of asking *what is that?* Likewise, the separation of related particles can easily lead the unwary translator into traps. This applies, in particular, to *ne . . . que*, meaning 'only', as the following example from a technical paper shows: *Pour simplifier, ces barres, tôles ou organes analogues ne sont representés que dans la figure 3.* (In order to simplify matters, these bars, sheets or similar members are shown in Fig. 3 only). A French text can look deceptively easy because of similarities in vocabulary, not all of which can, as we shall see later, be taken at their face value, but many translators experience great difficulties in translating it into English, this difficulty extending to a comparable extent to the other main Romance languages, i.e. Italian, Spanish and Portuguese. A good knowledge of French can be very helpful for translating Italian and Spanish and, to a lesser extent, Portuguese, at least on the information level. Romanian, very largely because of its geographical isolation, has departed farthest from its Latin parent, having borrowed extensively from the Slavonic and Finno-Ugric languages surrounding it. It is a language requiring special study and does not really benefit from an attempt at processes of triangulation. E. F. Bozman also has an amusing piece illustrating the nature of French from the translator's point of view, which I should like to quote here. "To translate from the French tongue is quite another thing. He has to it in the French tongue a clarity and lucidity who engages one to logical thought. It is necessary that one knows that which one wants to say, and then says it. With the French it is not necessary to say him two times; one time suffices. Through consequences, then, it is rigorous for the translator to decide what the author wants to say and having decided to select English words who will give him signification. This is not always easy because many of the English words have not of intention; nevertheless one cannot omit them. It is curious. By cause of this it is possible that the traducer loses that which there is to it of clarity within the mentality of the author. Precise thought, that exists not without precise expression; one can hope, nevertheless, that he who reads an English traduction of a French book can ordinarily obtain the original French, to the which he can refer when he wishes to discover that which the author wishes to say. The French books do not cost so dear as the English traductions."

When we come to consider the Slavonic languages, we are immediately confronted by additional difficulties. Although these languages belong to the same large Indo-

European family as the Germanic and Romance group, the
similarities are less apparent, added to which we do not
have the aid of German belonging to the same family as
English or of French having been derived from Latin.
Consequently, vocabulary learning is immediately made
more difficult in the case of the Slavonic languages. Added
to this, Russian and Bulgarian are written in the Cyrillic
alphabet which, although easy to learn to transliterate, is
not all that easy to visualize, particularly in the case of
long words, such as are liable to occur to quite a high
degree in these languages. Thirdly, all these Slavonic languages are fairly highly inflected and they also have a system
of aspects in verbs which is not found, at least in the same
way, in the other two main groups of languages spoken in
Europe. Also, the absence of a definite or indefinite article
in most Slavonic languages means that these have to be
supplied appropriately when translating into English. On
the other hand, there is the advantage that very many technical words in Russian and the other Slavonic languages
have been derived from Latin or Greek and thus form part
of the virtually universal vocabulary of science. Another
advantage is that many constructions found in Russian
have very close counterparts in German, so that translators
knowing German well will soon begin to feel certain affinities when they come to study Russian. Although Polish,
Czech and Slovak do not offer the difficulty of the Cyrillic
alphabet, they are little less inflected than Russian and are,
in any case, less important and useful as source languages,
so that this seeming initial advantage is, in the long run,
rather illusory. Compared with many languages used in
Europe, Russian is, however, extremely well documented
in relation to English by way of dictionaries, often of a
very specialized character, this being a great advantage to
the translator and one we shall be considering in greater
detail in the next chapter. For the sake of completeness,
we should perhaps quote E. F. Bozman's remarks about

Russian. "No one can read Russian. That is why their books must be translated. The Russian language is very queer. It is very much like English in many ways, but it has not the jollity of George Gissing or A. E. Housman. Go, little translator, and render the big Russian books into your little mother-tongue." As in most parodies, there is more than a grain of truth in those of Bozman.

Translation from such languages as Hungarian and Finnish, which belong, as we have said, to a completely different family from the majority of other languages already considered, presents considerable difficulties in that the structure of these languages differs greatly from that of Indo-European languages. The Finno-Ugric languages are, broadly speaking, based on what is called the agglutinative principle. This means that differences in meaning and in the function of words are indicated to a very large extent by the use of prefixes and suffixes. This often results in very long words containing more elements than the compound nouns already encountered in Germanic languages. For example, the Hungarian word for *unavoidably* is *elkerülhetetlenül*. Another feature of these languages is vowel harmony. This means that vowels of a certain quality only can occur in any given word and it also conditions the nature of the suffixes which can be added to that word. For example, in Hungarian, we find a word with low vowels and suffixes, such as *házamban* (in my house) and one with high vowels and suffixes, such as *kertemben* (in my garden). There is also the difficulty that the vocabulary in these languages is in no way related to that of the other Indo-European languages, nor is it very much related within the individual languages of the Finno-Ugric group, the similarities which do exist between these languages being restricted to the things that happen to words rather than the words themselves. It is interesting to note that the Finns themselves refer to their language as being the loneliest in Europe!

Translation from Japanese offers extreme difficulties, appreciated only by those who know something of the nature of the language. These difficulties arise mainly because of the system of writing used for Japanese, since it is, comparatively speaking, an easy language to speak, not having, for example, the tones found in many eastern languages, such as Chinese and Burmese. Written Japanese consists basically of two elements, namely characters for the most part taken over directly from Chinese, and two syllabaries, originally based on Chinese characters, but having been greatly simplified in form during the course of the centuries. One of these syllabaries—*hiragana*—is cursive in style and is used for indicating the various inflectional endings occurring in Japanese, while the other —*katakana*—is more angular in style and is used for the phonetic transcription of foreign words in Japanese, such as normally abound in, let us say, a chemical text. The finding of a given Chinese character in a Japanese-English dictionary is by no means as straightforward a process as, let us say, looking up a Portuguese word in a Portuguese-English dictionary. The Chinese characters are traditionally classified into any one of 214 groups and within these groups it is first necessary to decide to which group a given character belongs, based on the identification of the relevant radical. After having found the radical, it is then necessary to count the number of extra strokes involved in writing the character and, assuming all these steps have been carried out successfully, there is some possibility that the meaning of the character will be found! Japanese abounds in compounds and the same process has then to be adopted for finding them, added to which there are no spaces between words—in any case a vague concept in Japanese—so that it will be appreciated that the Japanese form of writing is probably the most complicated used today for a language of world importance. Various methods have been developed over the years for facilitating the identification of the relevant radical in a character. The system developed by Vaccari sets out to classify them according to their resemblance to the letters of our own alphabet, while that of Andrew Nelson, a missionary in Japan for many years, involves the successive use of twelve steps based on the position of key features in a character. Both systems alleviate the inherent difficulties, but neither eliminates them entirely. Coupled with these difficulties of basic identification, Japanese is an extremely vague language, not having the facility to pin-point many of the concepts we accept as being quite normal in most West European languages. Attempts to romanize Japanese have not prospered greatly and are, in any case, hampered by the large number of words in the language which sound the same, but which have different characters. Romanized textbooks can be used to learn to speak the language, but are of little assistance, except in the very early stages, if it is desired to learn to read it. Bearing in mind that very small differences in characters, such as a dot, can make all the difference between one meaning and another, it is essential that translators be provided with clear copies of Japanese texts, there even being something to be said for providing magnified copies. One concession that has been made in most, but not all, Japanese scientific journals and in all recent printed patent publications is that the characters—*kanji*—and *kana* are printed in lines from left to right and top to bottom and not in columns from right to left and top to bottom as in classical Japanese texts. As we have already said, the translator from Japanese in the United Kingdom cannot afford to specialize to the same extent as his colleagues working from West European languages, because of his scarcity value. He has to be omnivorous, much as he might wish to be vegetarian or carnivorous. We shall be having more to say about the training of translators from Japanese in Chapter IX.

We shall in the remainder of this chapter be considering

some of the specific problems facing translators in the case of texts from various European languages into English. These problems are of both a linguistic and non-linguistic character. Finally, we shall be looking at actual examples of translations.

(a) *Words that have to be omitted from or added to the translation*

One of the greatest difficulties for all translators, particularly in the early stages of their careers, is to escape, as it were, from the straitjacket of the original text from which they are translating. It probably follows from school exercises in translating from and into foreign languages that the original text is to be regarded as sacrosanct and inviolable. It is true that it should be regarded in this way, but it is a text the content and style of which have to be converted into another idiom, without necessarily preserving all the peculiarities native to the source text. This slavish following of the original often results in it being eminently clear to the reader that he is dealing with a translation and to a linguist that he is reading a translation made from language X, in much the same way as we can very often recognize the native tongue of a foreign speaker of English, partly through his accent and partly through the constructions he uses. Such a person is also very likely to use the same constructions when writing English, this being a good reason not to use him as a translator into it!

There are in most languages a number of small words or particles which belong to its correct usage, whereas they do not form part of the standard English idiom under the same circumstances. Examples from German include *schon, bekanntlich, sogenannt, noch, wissen Sie,* to mention but a few. This does not mean that these words can always be omitted in a translation, but they often can and should be, in some cases losing their original identity in the general tenor of the translation. Another such example, again from German, although it is restricted largely to the spoken language, is the seemingly impelling need to say "please" when handing someone something. If anything at all is said in English, it will usually be "here you are", but certainly not "please". In German, however, *bitte schön*, is perfectly correct. An example from Spanish is the preposition *a* used before certain nouns after a transitive verb. This obviously has to be omitted in a translation into English.

On the other hand, certain languages do not have words to express elements which we consider essential in good English. For example, Russian and Czech do not have any definite or indefinite article, such that the Czech word *matka* can mean "mother", "a mother" or "the mother", depending on the general context. It is, therefore, the task of the translator to insert "a(n)" or "the" where appropriate in his translation into English. Translations made by those of non-English mother-tongue from Czech and Russian into English can often be identified by failure to supply these articles. Similarly, languages such as German and Dutch very often do not use the indefinite article where it would be used in English. It too has then to be inserted as appropriate in the translation into English. Conversely, translators out of English into these languages have to make suitable omissions in such cases.

(b) *Faux amis*

This expression meaning literally "false friends", is used to describe those words in various languages which resemble in appearance words in other languages, but have a meaning quite different from the words they resemble. Examples of these are legion amongst most European languages and they represent one of the main stumbling blocks to inexperienced translators, particularly if their little knowledge has not taught them the dangers of guessing. It is good advice always to be on one's guard if a word is found, let us say, in French, which resembles an English word, since it may well be yet another "false friend". The translator has many true friends, and these should be cultivated rather than the false variety. Another case in which false friends are likely to be encountered is within the languages of any one family. Certain Dutch words bear a strong resemblance to certain German words, yet their meanings are quite different. Two notorious examples are Dutch *vertragen*, to slow down, slacken speed, and German *vertragen*, to endure, bear, and Dutch *betrachten*, to practise, exercise, and German *betrachten*, to examine, consider. Likewise, the Dutch word *particulier* means "private" in most cases, only occasionally meaning "particular" in the sense of "special". The German word *also* means "therefore", English "also" being *auch*. The French verb *demander* means "request" rather than "demand", this having given rise to much embarrassment in diplomatic circles on various occasions. The German word *Information*, when used in the plural, very often means "instructions" rather than "information". The Dutch word *conclusie*, particularly in a patent application or specification, means "claim" and not "conclusion" or "inference". If a piece of music is stated, in German, to be in *B*, this does not mean that it is in the key of B in English, but that of *B flat*. This error frequently occurs in translations on record sleeves. The French word *actuel* and its counterparts in German and Dutch means "topical" rather than "actual". Another notorious false friend of a similar type is the French *eventuel*, meaning "possible" rather than "eventual". Likewise the French *addition* means, at least in a restaurant, "bill" rather than "addition". Mention of "restaurant" reminds us that the Dutch word *restauratie* is used to describe a "refreshment room" on a station, for example, although it can in other contexts mean "restoration" or "renovation". The Spanish adjective *constipado* does not mean "constipated", but "having a cold in the head". The Danish word *Øl* does not mean "oil", as might be imagined from the German *Öl*, but "beer"! The Italian adjective *caldo* means "warm", and *morbido* means "soft", not "morbid". Hence to describe a girl as *calda e morbida* would be a compliment rather than the opposite.

These few examples will, it is hoped, have shown some of the pitfalls in translation that can arise from guessing that similar appearance implies similar or related meaning. The time taken to check such matters is, more often than not, amply repaid by certainty and accuracy in translation.

(c) *Words that cannot be "translated"*

A popular misconception, also amongst budding translators, is that any word in any language has a clear-cut equivalent in any other language. This is not in fact true, since some languages have concepts that are unknown to the people of another language. There are in most languages words that refer to concepts so specific to that language or the country in which it is spoken that they cannot be "translated", but have to be paraphrased or described. The English word *gentleman* and the expression *fair play* are to some extent examples of these, while the German word *Schadenfreude*, meaning that malicious type of enjoyment we sometimes derive from someone else's misfortune, such as the old man slipping on the banana skin, defies simple translation into English. Likewise, the German word *Einfühlung*, meaning the ability to feel oneself into the mind or feelings of another person in a given situation, is difficult to translate into English, unless we use the psychological term *empathy*. The German word *Festschrift*, being a volume of essays or papers written on the occasion of, let us say, the 60th birthday of a figure in the academic world, has no real counterpart in our own academic linguistic usage. Mention of the academic world reminds us of the difficulty of equating the various degrees and levels in the universities of different countries. Our own spectrum, ranging from assistant lecturer, lecturer, reader to professor, by no means has a direct counterpart in, let us say, the German-speaking academic world, so that functions such as those of *Lektor, ordentlicher Professor, ausserplanmässiger Professor, Dozent* and *Privatdozent* have to be described rather than translated. Likewise, certain European countries such as Germany and Austria, tend to use a large number of titles indicating functions and professions, and these too have to be described rather than translated. Examples are *Kammersänger* and *Obersanitätsrat*. Service ranks, too, present difficulties, as do the various titles for members of the nobility in various countries. These are not matters that many translators have to worry about, but some do, particularly when dealing with official documents. Confusion often arises, for example, in Dutch and English in that a lawyer in the Netherlands is addressed as *Meester*, having the abbreviation *Mr.* or *mr.*, this suggesting in English plain *Mr.* The Dutch academic title *Doctorandus*, abbreviated as *Drs.*, suggests to English people either that the person in question has two doctorates or that the proofreader has slipped up. Neither is the case, the title in fact meaning that the person in question has carried out all preliminary studies, etc. for obtaining a doctorate, but has not written and had accepted the necessary thesis. Difficulties of this type also occur sometimes in relation to the title of books. For example, the title of Zola's novel *Germinal* will mean very much more to an educated Frenchman than it will to the average Englishman, yet it is not translated, the English version of the work also being known as *Germinal*.

(d) *Foreign words*

There are no really pure languages, all containing a greater or lesser number of words which has been borrowed from other languages, with or without complete formal assimilation, not necessarily with a complete transfer of the original meaning. A distinction is made in German, for example, between a *Lehnwort* and a *Fremdwort*. Both have been borrowed from other languages, but the *Lehnwort* has been thoroughly assimilated and now shows no sign of its foreign origin, while the *Fremdwort* still betrays its foreign origin. It is with *Fremdwörter* that we are concerned here. A well-known German dictionary of such words runs to more than 30,000 entries, while there is a dictionary of similar proportions listing those used in Dutch. It is interesting to note, in passing, that these are both languages of countries which, in common with our own, do not have academies the task of which it is to review the language from time to time and to purge it, officially at least, of undesirable elements. The recent flood of British and American English words into French—France having such an academy!—has given rise to much concern and has led to the coining of the term *Franglais* to designate the resultant brand of French peppered with English words. Writers of advertising copy in many continental countries are notorious users of English or American words in their copy, such use often being associated with feelings of exclusivity and snobbism. The custom can, I suppose, be taken as a rather dubious compliment. The same idea no doubt lurks behind the use of a peculiar brand of French in ménus in various hotels and restaurants in England.

Translators of all categories are frequently confronted by foreign words, and the wider and more cosmopolitan their knowledge, the better they will be able to cope with them.

(e) *Regional differences*

Many of the languages we have been referring to in this chapter are not spoken or used in one country only. English, French, German, Dutch, Spanish and Portuguese are spoken in several countries or territories, often separated by many thousands of miles, while Russian is, as it were, the *lingua franca* of the inhabitants of several different Republics having, between them, a variety of indigenous languages. The English of, for example, England, Scotland, Australia, New Zealand and South Africa, not to mention that of the United States of America, is by no means the same, either in pronunciation, use of words and constructions, intonation, etc. The same also applies to the German of, let us say, West Germany, Austria and parts of Switzerland. This means, on the one hand, that the same concept may well have a different word used for it in Germany (possibly in West and East Germany), Austria and Switzerland, of which account must be taken when preparing, let us say, publicity literature for these countries. An examination of equivalent patent specifications will often reveal these regional differences in relation to technical words. On the other hand, the translator working into English must be informed whether a given text is intended for distribution in England or the United States, since he will have to modify his style, vocabulary and spelling accordingly. It is also interesting to note in this context that the large waves of immigrants to the United States from various Central European countries have had an influence on American technical vocabulary, possibly to a greater extent than they have on British English. This can be noticed in music, for example, where the Americans tend to use fractional names for the length of notes, while we in England still adhere to *minims* and *quavers*. A continental influence on American space-exploration vocabulary could also probably be established.

Another point worthy of attention is that in certain countries there is quite often a distinct difference between the spoken and written language. There are, for example, in Dutch several "book words" which have their "spoken" counterparts. Such differences must, of course, be appreciated by translators of texts which are intended to be spoken rather than read, such as those of plays and works for television and radio, as well as films.

Dialect and slang also present the translator with great difficulties. Should these be translated into what seem their counterparts in the target language or should they be suppressed, thus altering the atmosphere and register and possibly also dispensing with their function as indicators of social differences in, let us say, a play or film? These are questions which the translator of literary works in particular has to consider. Few countries perhaps go as far as English in the direction of U and non-U elements, as set out, for example, in *Noblesse Oblige*, edited by Nancy Mitford. There are, however, obvious centres of good and bad linguistic usage in all countries and they constitute an element which cannot be ignored in translating. This is also one further reason why a translator should have an up-to-date knowledge of the source and target languages with which he is dealing. This involves not only wide reading at all levels, but also, if at all possible, regular visits to the countries concerned. This is one reason why English-speaking translators working on the Continent are encouraged to visit England periodically, in order to remain conversant with current linguistic usage. You can, for example, imagine the brand of English which would be spoken or written by someone who had gained his sole knowledge of it from reading the works of Dickens or Thackeray! This recalls the habit of Hitler's chief interpreter, Paul Schmidt who, in his book *Statist auf diplomatischer Bühne* mentions his indebtedness to radio broadcasts for keeping his vocabulary up to date in his various languages.

(f) *Translation of proper names*

This offers difficulties to the translator in that certain languages do not have certain sounds and, consequently,

when representing names incorporating those sounds have
to resort to a compromise and use the nearest sound available in their language. On the other hand, some languages
need use but one letter to represent a sound requiring two
or three letters in another language. These two processes
can give rise to the appearance of proper names in forms
in which they will not be immediately recognized. For
example, the name of the Russian composer Чайковский
can take the following forms in various West European
languages: English: *Tchaikovsky*; German: *Tschaikowsky*;
Dutch: *Tsjaikowskij*; French: *Tchaïkowsky*; Hungarian:
Csajkovszkij; Czech: *Čajkovskij*. Conversely, such West
European names as *Hill* and *Walton* have to be transliterated
as Хилл and Уолтон in Russian, since the language does
not have the sounds represented by our *h* and *w*. It may
seem ironic that the name of George Bernard Shaw, who
was so much in favour of reforming the English alphabet,
should appear in Russian simply as Шоу.

Japanese, too, is lacking in certain sounds, principally *r*
and *v* (although a *katakana* symbol has been introduced
for the latter sound when transliterating foreign names
incorporating it). This fact and other peculiarities of Japanese often give rise to barely recognizable forms of western
firms when they are transliterated back from their Japanese
kana forms into English either by Japanese or English
translators. The following are typical examples of the process: *Falbwelke Hext Aktiengesellshaft, folmars Meister
Rutius und Blewning (Farbwerke Hoechst Aktiengesellschaft,
vormals Meister Lucius und Brüning), Fabenfabriken Beil
AG (Farbenfabriken Bayer AG)* and *Eastoman Koduck
Company (Eastman Kodak Company).*

In addition to these more obvious difficulties, translators
must also realize that, in Hungarian, the surname is placed
first, followed by the christian name. Thus, the Hungarian
form of my own name would be *Finlay Ian*. This method
is, on reflexion, much more logical than our own, in that

E

there are far fewer people with the surname *Finlay* than there are with the christian name *Ian*, and it is better to establish that I am a *Finlay* rather than that I am an *Ian*. Russian and Japanese names also require careful handling by translators, as do those of married women in the Netherlands in the case of which the woman's maiden name is coupled with that of her husband. Strangely enough, it is seemingly minor matters of this type that often tend to be omitted from courses of instruction for linguists in general.

(g) *Trade marks and slogans*

These offer difficulties to the translator in two main ways. Firstly, he must be able to recognize a word as a trade mark and not as a generic word and, secondly, it does not by any means always follow that, because a word is a trade mark in one country, it will also be in other countries in which it is used. The word *nylon*, for example, is in most countries a generic word denoting a particular class of polyamide fibres, but it is a trade mark in France and should, therefore, be written in a distinctive manner in French texts, in order to distinguish it from other generic words for fibres, such as *laine* (wool) or *coton* (cotton). On the other hand, the word *Terylene* is a registered trade mark in almost every country having a provision for the registration of trade marks and should, therefore, always be treated as such in a text. It is, incidentally, also registered in certain non-Roman scripts, including Cyrillic, then appearing as Терилен. This also serves to illustrate a point to which reference has already been made, namely that when choosing a trade mark for international use, it is as well to arrive at one which can be used in all countries without conflicting too greatly with local orthography. From this point of view, *Kodak* and *Coca-Cola* are little short of brilliant. The latter can and also has been transliterated quite successfully into the special scripts used for such languages as Gujarati, Hindi, Thai, Urdu, Greek, Amharic and Chinese!

There is often the tendency on the part of some countries to adapt trade marks to their own linguistic context or usage. Thus, the trade mark *Terylene* tends, in France, to be written as *Térylène*. This is, however, incorrect practice, since the word is registered in France as *Terylene*. The practice is obviously analogous to that of the German saying "please" when handing one something.

Certain patented processes carried out in various countries can occasionally appear as "foreign" verbs in the languages of those countries. A good example of this is the word *sanforise* (referring to a textile finishing treatment). It appears as *sanforisieren* in German, *sanforiseren* in Dutch and *sanforiser* in French.

The correct use of trade marks in translations, particularly of the publicity or prestige variety, is very important, since they tend to lose or run the risk of losing their legal status as trade marks unless they are treated in a distinctive manner, as more than one manufacturer has learnt to his cost over the years. Examples of "lost" trade marks include linoleum, gramophone, cellophane and escalator.

The translation of slogans belongs in many ways more to the sphere of the copywriter than to that of the translator, although the latter will often be called in to make such translations, usually at the last minute! The quality of a slogan can make or mar the chances of a new product on a new market, and its "translation"—"adaptation" would be a better word—calls for a knowledge extending far beyond a pure translation. Certain slogans adapt remarkably well to a variety of languages. Two examples come to mind, namely the wording used in conjunction with the *Wool Mark* and the phrase used in conjunction with the launching of the new *Ford Capri*. The latter sounds as well in German as it did in English, i.e. *Der Capri, das Auto, das Sie sich schon immer gewünscht haben.*

There will be found on garments made from pure new wool, provided with the *Wool Mark* in France *Pure laine vierge*, in Germany *Reine Schur-Wolle*, in the Netherlands *Zuiver Scheerwol* and in Sweden *Ren ny ul*.

(h) *Abbreviations*

Abbreviations and acronyms, that is to say words made up from the initial letters of, for example, an organization, present formidable problems to the translator and jointly constitute possibly the greatest time-wasting factor in all his work. Abbreviations are often formed quite arbitrarily by authors to whom it never occurs to imagine that others may not be members of their own private worlds. Editors of journals, particularly of the scientific or technical variety, could well perform a more useful function in this respect, insisting either that standard abbreviations only are used or that a list of all abbreviations used in an article is appended to it. Writers of reports, too, are often guilty of inflicting their private shorthand unexplained on their readers. There are many dictionaries of abbreviations and acronyms in many languages. Some are excellent, such as the *Abkürzungs-lexikon*, compiled by Paul Spillner for German. It contains well over 35,000 entries covering a very wide field and has solved many a problem for me. It has not, however, been able to solve such problems as *LHSV*, meaning "liquid hourly space velocity" or *Hi-Bi-Prozess*, meaning *hohe Doppelbrechung-Prozess* or, in plain English, "process resulting in the formation of filaments having a high degree of birefringence". I can well understand why the term was coined, but I do wish it had been explained as well. Abbreviations are, of course, more likely to be found in technical than in literary texts and, as suggested, can often be very hard nuts to crack, although the solution frequently seems simple once one has it.

Acronyms abound in our modern world. Here are a few

examples taken at random from a variety of European languages: *Oxfam, Unesco, Aslib, Adac, Horeca, DAW, EFTA, Pluto* and *TAS*. In this case, I shall leave readers to puzzle them out for themselves. They cover English, German, Dutch and Russian.

The moral to be drawn from all this is that use of abbreviations and acronyms should be kept to a minimum and that, if they are or have to be used, they should be explained fully on their first occurrence. This would save translators and others more time and trouble than the adoption of the metric system!

(i) *Changes in orthography*

A number of European and other languages has made greater or lesser changes, usually in the direction of simplifications and consistencies, in orthography during the past hundred years or so. This inevitably means that the translator will be confronted with texts exhibiting various spellings and that, if he is using old dictionaries, he will in some cases have to make allowances for changes in spelling when looking up certain words. He will also find that many older German texts and dictionaries will be printed in Gothic or *Fraktur* type, this sometimes also being the case with Danish.

Amongst the many languages which have had greater or lesser changes in orthography are German, Dutch, Danish, Portuguese, Hungarian and Russian. German has in certain words replaced *th* by *t*, as in *Thür* and *Thier* which are now written *Tür* and *Tier*. Dutch has had innumerable spelling changes over the years, this being a source of continual annoyance to those who were educated under one system, only now to find that they have to readjust themselves to a new system. Such changes in spelling are, of course, also associated with emotional overtones, since they can also affect personal names and, very often, street names and the like. Most of the changes in Dutch relate to the dropping of superfluous double vowels, as in *roode* which has become *rode* or *heeren* which has now become *heren*, or to the spelling of some of the many words that the Dutch have taken over from other languages, such as *succes* which now appears as *sukses*, much to the horror of many Dutchmen and others! In some respects Dutch spelling has been moving in the direction of that of Afrikaans (which developed from Dutch), although this latter language has carried the process of the elimination of letters to a very much greater extent. Here are a few examples: Dutch: *nieuwste*; Afrikaans: *nuuste*; D.: *samengesteld*; A.: *saamgestel*; D.: *hoogst*; A.: *hoogs*. The changes in Danish refer both to the dropping of Gothic or *Fraktur* type, the giving up of the custom of writing all nouns with an initial capital letter, as is still done in German, and to changing the order of the letters of the alphabet and, consequently, of dictionary entries. Formerly *Aa* was the first letter of the Danish alphabet, words beginning with this letter, such as *aabne* (to open), appearing at the beginning of a dictionary. This letter is now written as *Å*, and words beginning with it will now be found at the very end of a dictionary. Changes in Hungarian have been of a minor character, affecting for the most part only the letter *cz* which is now written *c*. Thus *ceruza* (pencil) used to be written *czeruza* and will be found as such in older dictionaries dating from the earlier part of the nineteenth century. In 1918, the Russian revolutionary government dispensed with certain letters, and these are, of course, still likely to be encountered in pre-revolutionary texts and dictionaries.

Changes in orthography have not been restricted to West European languages. Perhaps the most far-reaching change of all was the adoption of the Roman alphabet for writing Turkish, a form of Arabic script having been used for Turkish prior to the innovation of Kemal Ataturk in 1928. Certain Japanese characters, too, have been simplified following the end of World War II, and there has been a restriction on those that may be used in newspapers and certain other types of literature. Most scientific texts in Japanese are now printed in rows from left to right, rather than in columns from right to left as used to be the case for all Japanese texts.

Finally, in this section, differences in spelling between British and American English have increased in recent years, these affecting a number of technical words. Examples are *sulfur* and *aluminum* which are, in British English, *sulphur* and *aluminium*. The symbols for these two elements —*S* and *Al*—are, however, universal.

(j) *Handwriting*

Although most texts which translators receive are these days typed or printed, a translator from, let us say, German, will look very foolish if he cannot translate a letter in German handwriting merely because he cannot read it! The same applies to Russian, Yiddish and Hebrew as well as to Japanese. The moral of this is that a translator worthy of the name should make sure that he obtains practice in reading the handwritten forms of his source languages. This, too, is a point that is frequently overlooked in training courses.

(k) *Bibliographical references*

These frequently occur at the end of articles in journals, and ways of indicating them frequently differ from country to country. These differences relate to such matters as volume number, year, issue within a year and the like. For the sake of uniformity, it is desirable that the translator should adopt the system current in the country of the target language. British Standard 1629 : 1950 deals with Biblio-graphical References and should form part of every scientific translator's library. It covers books, periodicals and various ancillary matters.

The translator has also to decide whether to translate into the target language the names of foreign book or article titles. If these are translated—and this seems advisable—it is preferable to indicate that the text in question has not necessarily been translated into the target language. References in Cyrillic type and those in Japanese will also have to be transliterated into the Roman alphabet. The Cyrillic alphabet no longer offers any great difficulties in this respect, any more than does Greek, but we have already referred in section (f) of this chapter to the difficulties that are encountered in the case of Japanese. There is, in fact, also a British Standard covering the transliteration of Cyrillic and Greek characters (British Standard 2979 : 1958).

(l) *Conversion of units*

Unfortunately, not all countries yet use the same units for the same quantities. Even although time is virtually universally expressed in hours, minutes and seconds, both the Japanese and Jews have their own system of chronology for indicating years. Those dealing with Japanese patent publications must consequently be able to convert the year of *Showa* (the 1st year of *Showa* was 1926, being the year of accession of the present Emperor, so that 1970 is the 45th year of *Showa*) into the corresponding year in western chronology.

Units of length, area, volume and weight very often have to be converted and such conversions can become quite complicated, such as, for example, when a double conversion is involved as in kilometres per litre to miles per gallon. There are several systems used for indicating the thickness or weight of textile fibres and yarns, although a universal system, using a unit called a *tex*, is gradually being adopted. These textile conversions can be very complicated too, so that translators working in this field should obtain a set of conversion tables.

Translators will also often be expected to convert costs from one currency to another, since a price of 20 roubles, for example, will mean little to average English readers of a translation.

All these may seem minor points, but they contribute to creating the impression on the reader that he is *not* reading a translation.

(m) *Tables*

Many technical papers include complicated tables which the translator will have to cope with, probably on an *ad hoc* basis. Problems of setting out and spacing are best left to a professional typist, but the translator must ensure that all elements in the tables have been translated or "converted" into a form usual in the country of the target language.

Captions to figures will also have to be dealt with, either by providing a legend, keying by numbers or possibly by removing the captions in the source language and replacing them by the equivalents in the target language. "House style" and the customer's wishes will probably be the deciding factor here. Many customers rightly like to have the tables and illustrations inserted at appropriate places in the translation, while others do not object if they are all relegated to the end of the translation. It is here a case of *chacun à son goût*, but the translator must be prepared to co-operate. Some firms issue very elaborate lists of instructions relating to the treatment of tables and illustrations in translations.

(n) *Numbers*

It might be thought that numbers would offer no problems in translations, but this is far from the case. In most continental countries a full stop is used to separate thousands, whereas a comma is used instead of our decimal point. Thus, 30.93 becomes 30,93 in, let us say, a German text, while 300,000 can appear in a German text as 300.000 or sometimes as 300 000 or even 300'000, this latter form sometimes being encountered in Switzerland. Thus 7'234,77 according to our system, would in fact be 7,234.77. I recently encountered in a Spanish text the following method of typing "August 1949" *Agosto de* 1.949.

British, American and continental usage also differs in some cases in relation to the terms used for very high numbers. For example, the German *Milliarde* means, in British English, a *thousand million* whereas, in American English it is a *billion*! Such high numbers may not mean much to most of us, but they can make all the difference between a contract seeming interesting or uninteresting to a firm contemplating a merger.

Translators should also know how to read numbers, squares, square roots and the like in their source and target languages, since they may well be asked to do this from time to time. This again is something that tends to be neglected in most training courses.

(o) *Chemical formulae*

These, because of their virtual universality, offer few real difficulties. An equation such as $NaOH + HCl \rightarrow NaCl + H_2O$ will be equally intelligible to a Russian, Japanese or American chemist. Conventions can sometimes differ in the naming of complex organic compounds, but there are books describing the methods accepted in a given country or used in a given publication. It is, therefore, up to the translator to make himself familiar with them. It may be worth pointing out that it is possible to obtain plastic stencils that can be used for drawing the outline of benzene rings and other outlines frequently occurring in the structural formulae of organic compounds. These too should form part of the chemical translator's equipment, as should, of course, such elementary instruments as a compass and a set square.

The above are some of the many matters to which the translator must devote his attention, if he is to be regarded as a fully professional practitioner of his art and craft. There are, of course, other matters, and no two translations will ever be quite the same in the problems they pose. This again is a pleasing aspect of the translator's work, comparable in many ways to that of his other professional colleagues, such as solicitors, barristers, doctors and dentists, to whom likewise no two cases or operations will be quite the same. After all, they are all dealing with human beings or products of the human mind, and no two human beings are quite alike.

Finally, to conclude this long chapter, we shall look at a few examples of translations. These will, of necessity, be short, but will indicate some of the points in action to which we have referred in theory in this and other chapters.

The first example concerns two prose and four verse translations of the first verse of Charles Baudelaire's poem *L'Albatros*, taken from his collection *Les Fleurs du Mal*. These will indicate the types of results obtained by the two methods by which the translating of poetry can be carried out.

Here is Baudelaire's original:

> Souvent, pour s'amuser, les hommes d'équipage
> Prennent des albatros, vastes oiseaux des mers,
> Qui suivent, indolents compagnons de voyage,
> Le navire glissant sur les gouffres amers.

As will be seen, the language itself is not difficult, so that the translator can concentrate fully on using his skill in transferring the text from French into English, firstly in prose and then in verse.

The first prose translation is that by Anthony Hartley, taken from *The Penguin Book of French Verse: (3) The Nineteenth Century*. It reads as follows:

> Often to amuse themselves, the men of the crew trap albatrosses, the great sea-birds, that follow the ship slipping over the bitter deeps, like idle travelling companions.

The second prose translation is that by Francis Scarfe from the Baudelaire volume of *The Penguin Poets*. It reads as follows:

> Often, for their amusement, sailors catch albatross, those vast birds of the sea, indolent companion of their voyages, that follow the ship gliding across the bitter depths.

Both these prose translations give the sense of Baudelaire's original quite adequately. There are differences, such as "great" as opposed to "vast" to describe the size of the albatross, and "idle" as opposed to "indolent", but these are more matters of personal choice. The change from verse to prose is, however, immediately evident as are the differences in timbre between the French original and the English translations. All that has been preserved is the sense of the original (this, however, being the one essential element if we are considering the poem as a vehicle for communication). It can, of course, also be regarded as a vehicle for communicating much more in addition, such as mood, images, etc.

Let us now look at the four verse translations. The first is by C. F. MacIntyre, an American translator:

> Sometimes, sailors to amuse themselves
> catch albatrosses, great birds of the sea,
> which as companions follow indolently
> the vessel gliding over bitter gulfs.

It will first of all be noted that MacIntyre has dispensed with the rhymes, occurring in the original between the 1st

and 3rd and 2nd and 4th lines. Likewise, the function of
the word *indolents* in the original has been changed from
an adjective to an adverb, while *souvent* has had its meaning
restricted from "often" to "sometimes". Finally, "gulfs"
can hardly be said to be an accurate translation for *gouffres*
in this context. It can mean "gulfs", but surely "depths"
is more in keeping with the mood of the poem. Consequently, we have lost the rhymes, had the sense distorted
somewhat, but gained little in any other way.

The next verse translation is that by Roy Campbell:

> Sometimes for sport the men of loafing crews
> Snare the great albatrosses of the deep,
> The indolent companions of their cruise
> As through the bitter vastitudes they sweep.

Here the rhymes have been preserved, but once again
we find that this has taken place at a cost. The word
"loafing" has been added to the meaning of the original.
It might be reasonable to assume it, but it is not in the original. The word "cruise" hardly describes mid-nineteenth
century voyages and suggests something very different from
Baudelaire's intention. "Vastitudes" is a fine word and this
last line is worthy of inclusion in any poem, be it an
original or a translation. This translation can, therefore,
be considered more successful than that by MacIntyre.

The third verse translation is that by Alan Conder:

> In sport a vessel's crew will often take
> The mighty albatross, who on the breeze
> Doth idly sail and follow in the wake
> Of ships that glide upon the bitter seas.

Again the rhyming pattern has been preserved. "Mighty"
is an appropriate translation for *vastes*, but the introduction
of the concept of "breeze" is foreign to the original. This
translation takes greater liberties with the sense of the
original than did that by Roy Campbell, so that it is, in

my opinion, less successful on the whole than Campbell's.

Finally, here is another verse translation by another American translator, Wallace Fowlie:

> Often, as an amusement, crewmen
> Catch albatrosses, huge birds of the sea,
> Who follow, indolent companions of the voyage,
> The ship gliding over the salty deeps.

The rhymes have been omitted here. The sense has been preserved pretty well. "Salty" is a reasonable translation for *amers*, in that the bitter taste of sea water is due to the salt it contains. "Crewmen" sounds a little strange to our ears, however, There is the impression here that, as in the case of MacIntyre's translation, little has been gained by setting out the translation in the form of verse over and above what a professed prose translation would have produced. Summing up, then, we can say that both the prose translations are thoroughly adequate, bearing in mind that they were produced to follow the word order and sense of the original as closely as possible, and that Roy Campbell's verse translation is the most successful and satisfying of the four, both as a translation of Baudelaire's original and as a poem in its own right. It is not unreasonable to invoke this last criterion since a poem must be evaluated as such, whatever its origin.

Finally, I give my own prose translation of the verse, departing a little from the strict following of the word order of the original in the two translations given above:

> In order to amuse themselves, the members of the crew often catch albatrosses, those huge sea-birds which, as indolent companions on the voyage, follow the ship gliding over the bitter depths.

An important point to be considered in any evaluation of translations of verse is the dividing line between a criticism or assessment of the translation as a translation and that of the result from the point of view of literary criticism. We have, I think, correctly stressed the former criterion.

To conclude, there follow a few random examples chosen from technical texts. Firstly, here is a sentence from a Russian paper, followed by the translation as originally produced—for information—and an improved version:

> В течение последних лет в нашей стране и за рубежом проводятся работы по применению в шинах корда повышенной толщины, что позволяет снизить слойность каркаса.

During the course of last Summer in our country and abroad there was carried out work on the application in tyres of cord of increased thickness, which allowed a lowering in the number of plies of the carcass.

Work was carried out during the summer of 1967, both in Russia and elsewhere, on the use in tyres of cord of increased thickness, this allowing the number of plies in the carcass to be reduced.

Here are two different versions of an information translation from German:

> Man wird nämlich nicht nur polare Fasern aus wässrigen und wenig polare aus Lösungsmittel-Flotten färben, sondern man färbt schon heute auch synthetische Fasern aus wässrigen Flotten.

Because not only are polar fibres dyed in aqueous baths and sparingly polar ones in solvent baths, but nowadays synthetic fibres may already be dyed in aqueous baths also.

For example, not only polar fibres will be dyed from aqueous liquors and slightly polar fibres from solvent liquors, but in fact synthetic fibres are being dyed from aqueous liquors.

The original German is not of the highest order, but the second translator has coped better with the problems posed by the original.

Finally, here is a choice example of what can result if people either write in or translate into a language which is not their mother-tongue. It can be assumed that the producer of this had Polish as mother-tongue:

> We wish to call your attention to the fact that this term is a deadline. In case the prior art will not be filed at least on December 10th, 1969, the above mentioned application shall be undone.

It is reasonably clear what is meant, but not entirely so. A better version might be:

> We should like to point out that this is a final date, and should an account of the prior art not be filed by 10th December, 1969 at the latest, the above-mentioned application will be rejected.

All these examples illustrate, to a greater or lesser extent, the danger to which the translator is always exposed, namely that of following the original too closely. The original must, of course, be used as the basis for the translation, but it must be assimilated by the translator and then reproduced in reconstituted form, the reconstituted form being adapted to the new medium. It is in this way only that a smooth translation can be produced rather than one that is only too obviously a translation. The last line of Baudelaire's poem *L'Albatros* is not inappropriate to quote in this context: *Ses ailes de géant l'empêchent de marcher*. The original should never prevent the translator from producing a smooth translation. There is a marked difference between a good and a bad translation, sufficient, I hope, to show that translation is both a craft and an art involving the manipulation of words, which can often be highly intractable. There are coherent and incoherent translations just as there is coherent and incoherent speech. There are pedestrian and virtuoso translations just as there are pedestrian and virtuoso performances of a musical work.

It is hoped that these few examples, in conjunction with the various other points considered earlier in the chapter, will have given readers some idea of what goes on in the translator's study or office between the receipt of a text for translation and the delivery of the finished product. As we implied at the beginning of the chapter, translating cannot be taught entirely, although it is possible to guide people in the direction of perfection rather than allowing them to remain in the area of mediocrity. It is only by knowing the pitfalls that one can hope to avoid them. There was much truth in Oscar Wilde's saying that the purpose of art was to conceal art.

READING LIST

Edwards, P. M. H.—*Problems in Typing Foreign-Language Material*. The Incorporated Linguist, October 1965, pp. 104-106.

Foreign-Language Printers.—The Incorporated Linguist, October 1964, pp. 103-109.

Henn, A. K.—*Scientific Translation from Japanese*. The Incorporated Linguist, October 1963, pp. 117-120.

Macandrew, R. M.—*Translation from Spanish*. London 1936.

Podborny, J. G.—*Zu einer international einheitlichen Umschreibung der kyrillischen Buchstaben*. Babel, Vol. V, No. 4, December 1959, pp. 207-212.

Readett, A. G. and Oakland, W. H.—*How does Translation affect the Length of a Text?* The Incorporated Linguist, October 1963, pp. 102-112.

Ritchie, R. L. G.—*Translation from French*. Cambridge 1923.

Viragh, Z.—*Übersetzung und Anpassung von Warenzeichen*. Weinheim 1966.

CHAPTER VI

THE TRANSLATOR'S TOOLS OF TRADE

In common with most artists and craftsmen, the translator has his tools of trade, in other words, a variety of aids which assist him in his work. It should not, however, be thought that good and profuse tools necessarily ensure good work or that a lack of these implies poor work, since the contribution made by the translator himself remains possibly the most important factor governing the quality of his work. Nevertheless, there are many things which can help the translator, and he would be foolish not to avail himself of them to the full. These aids may be divided roughly into linguistic and literary aids and mechanical aids of various types. We shall be considering them in detail in this chapter.

(a) *Linguistic aids*

These include dictionaries, glossaries and grammars. I hope, however, that it has already become apparent that these are not the sole aids a translator requires, this being a view still prevalent amongst some non-linguists!

Dictionaries started their life many centuries ago when the need arose to explain in various vernaculars certain words occurring, for example, in works in Latin which would not otherwise have been intelligible to the ordinary people. It is, in this regard, tempting to think that the wheel has just about turned full circle when, for example, one feels constrained to ask one's solicitor just what some of the terms occurring in the deeds of the house one is buying mean. A perusal of the title of some of the contributions to a journal such as "Nature" is likely to produce the same reaction on the non-subject specialist. The origin of dictionaries was, then, the glossing of early manuscripts for the benefit of the common people in a given linguistic group. Carried to its ultimate degree, this produced what is called an interlinear version of, let us say, the original Latin text in the respective vernacular, in other words, the earliest bilingual version. A collation of the words which had been glossed, arranged in alphabetical order, resulted in the first bilingual dictionaries which, interestingly enough, very often preceded monolingual dictionaries. The word "glossary", about which we shall be saying more later, has obviously preserved its relationship with the principle of "glossing" rather than dictionary-making.

From these distant times, the battery of dictionaries now available to the translator has grown to alarming proportions, today covering such types as monolingual, bilingual, poly- or multilingual, illustrated and various other specialized categories. Obviously, not all dictionaries are equally good, nor are they all equally suitable or appropriate for a given purpose.

Monolingual dictionaries, such as *Brockhaus* for German, *Larousse* for French and the Concise Oxford for English, are ideal in the right hands as general dictionaries of the languages in question in that they explain the meaning of words in those languages and indicate what they mean to the inhabitants of the country having that language as their mother tongue. Thus, all translators should have a dictionary of the monolingual type for their various source languages and they should, during training, be encouraged and taught to use them at the earliest possible opportunity.

General dictionaries, be they of the mono-, bi- or multilingual type, are of secondary importance to most technical translators, although they are useful to and necessary for most general and literary translators. What most technical and scientific translators desire more than anything is a dictionary that will tell them more and more about less and less. Better, for example, a list of one hundred items referring to the drawing of synthetic fibres, than a general textile dictionary containing only a quarter of such items. A highly specialized list of this type is the very opposite of dictionaries such as Patterson's excellent German/English and French/English dictionaries for chemists, both of which contain general as well as more specialized vocabulary. They even contain parts of the verb "to be" and are, in this way, ideal for the "do-it-yourself" chemist/translator in that he needs one dictionary only which will provide him with a high percentage of the words he is likely to encounter in general chemical texts.

There are now several dictionaries incorporating a number of different languages, but covering fairly closely circumscribed technical fields. These can be very useful to the technical translator working from a number of source languages, although some can be rather cumbersome to use because of the cross-indexing systems used. They also have the advantage that one is, as it were, obtaining as many as six dictionaries in one, the price by no means being six times that of just one dictionary within the subject field in question. Certain of these dictionaries also provide definitions in the basic language.

Mention of definitions brings us to glossaries which, as we have implied, differ in general from dictionaries in that they present a selection only of the words in a language, ideally giving the words within a very restricted field only. Glossaries are being produced to an ever increasing extent today, either in the form of books or as what are called "hidden" glossaries in various linguistic journals. We shall be having more to say about these later. An excellent glossary is that prepared by Gunston and Corner covering financial and economic terms in German and English. Its main advantage, apart from the fact that it contains innumerable terms not already in dictionaries, is that it gives examples of the German terms in context, in other words in the form in which translators are likely to encounter them in texts. It would be wonderful if translators could have at their disposal works of this type for many more languages and subjects. Unfortunately, such works are still few and far between.

There are also many illustrated dictionaries, particularly in technical spheres. A good example are the now rather old *Schlomann-Oldenbourg* multilingual illustrated technical dictionaries. Most of these are now getting on for fifty years old, but they are still very useful in many fields in which there have not been revolutionary changes, such as, for example, the processing of natural fibres, such as cotton and wool. Some dictionaries also have illustrated supplements.

Contrary to popular opinion, dictionaries and glossaries do not provide anything like all the answers to vocabulary problems. They cannot even always be relied upon to be accurate and they are always, by their very nature, out of date when they appear. There is a saying that the method of the dictionary-maker is to crib as much as possible from his predecessors! This is obviously an exaggeration, although it is interesting to see in some cases how the error of one lexicographer has been perpetuated by his successors. Some dictionaries are extremely dangerous in that they offer merely lists of seeming synonyms, without indicating the specific technical sphere in which the word has each of the possible meanings listed. One German/English technical dictionary gives close on fifty meanings for the word *Ansatz*, with little if any indication as to when each of them is an appropriate equivalent. As we have mentioned, dictionaries are sometimes prepared by those who will have to use them, in other words translators, but cases are also known in which they are prepared by people very much divorced from the reality and practice of translating. In the case of dictionaries, there is much to be said for a review prior to publication rather than after!

Important, too, in dictionaries is the way in which they are set out. A clearly set-out dictionary, printed on good quality paper, the pages of which lie flat on a desk can be a joy to use compared with one printed on poor paper which also has to be held open and in which it is difficult to differentiate between the individual entries. This all suggests that there is still much work to be done on the production of dictionaries for those who are to use them.

Bearing in mind the number and cost of dictionaries and glossaries, it is often quite impossible for the private translator to acquire all that he might want or need. A figure of at least £50 a year has been suggested as a reasonable sum for the free-lance to spend on dictionaries. He should, therefore, examine reviews of new dictionaries appearing in the various linguistic journals and should, if possible, inspect them and, ideally, use them on an appropriate text before deciding to purchase. Dictionaries, in common with most reference books, are difficult to borrow, but there is an excellent collection, particularly in the technical field, in the Patent Office Library in London and in the library of the Institute of Linguists, also in London. The public has access to the former library, and members of the Institute to the latter.

No translator can know or remember all the subtleties of the grammar of all the languages he may be called upon to translate from. This applies particularly to information translators working for industrial firms who are often required to translate material from languages they may not know all that intimately. In such cases, a comprehensive and reliable reference grammar of the languages in question is, to say the least, desirable. These too may therefore be considered as a legitimate tool of trade for the translator.

Another purely linguistic aid for the translator is a dictionary of synonyms for his target language and also, if possible, for his various source languages. It has been stated that there are no true synonyms. Be this as it may, a volume such as Peter Roget's *Thesaurus of English Words and Phrases* together with its counterparts in various other languages can be a very useful aid for deciding on the correct word or expression in a given context. Such volumes are the constant companions of some of the best writers.

Not all languages or subjects are equally well linked through dictionaries and other linguistic works of reference, this factor being taken into account in the assessment of translating rates as we shall be seeing in Chapter VIII. It by no means follows, for example, that those languages from which translations into English will often be required are best documented in relation to English. This applies to French, for example, which is notoriously badly documented in relation to English in the sphere of specialized technical dictionaries. German and Russian are, on the other hand, fairly well documented in relation to English, as is Hungarian. Although there are some excellent Japanese/English dictionaries of a general nature, there is a distinct shortage when it comes to certain specialized fields. It will frequently be found that translators will use, when dealing with, let us say, a translation from Swedish into English, not a Swedish/English dictionary, but a Swedish/German dictionary, mentally translating the German into English. This is, I suppose, an example of the linguistic pyrotechnics indulged in by the translator or linguist, although it is sometimes dictated by the shortage or unavailability of suitable reference works in a given field linking the languages involved.

Summarizing this section on dictionaries and other linguistic aids for the translator, the best advice that can be given is to choose and use the most suitable dictionary for a given translation.

(b) *Subject-matter and literature aids*

In addition to occasional linguistic aids, the translator will also, and possibly more importantly in the case of advanced new techniques and processes, require subject-matter aids. These take the form of technical encyclopaedias and works of reference in his various source languages and target language as well as relevant periodicals in these languages covering his various subject specializations. It is frequently not realized by non-linguists that translators should spend quite a deal of their time keeping up with the latest developments in their specialized spheres. It is for this reason that many technical translators find the television programme *Tomorrow's World* so useful. Likewise, a translator specializing in medical texts will probably be found to be a regular reader of a publication such as *The Lancet*. The translator will have to consult libraries, since he cannot afford too large or expensive a library of his own. There are many libraries scattered throughout the country with good specialized collections of technical literature, some of which have borrowing facilities. The growth in the photo-copying facilities offered by many reference libraries is also something that the translator should consider. Copyright problems seldom arise here, if the documents copied are required for private study or research. The translator working in industry or for a research organization will have the advantage of direct access to the libraries normally attached to such bodies.

There are many potential aids to the translator in the sphere of literature. These include translations of foreign standards, a large number of which is available for consultation or borrowing from the British Standards Institution in London. Several multilingual publications, such as the journal *Endeavour*, produced by Imperial Chemical Industries Limited, *Soviet Union*, the *DDR Review*, *Reader's Digest*, to mention but a few, can on occasions be

remarkably useful to the translator, in that they enable him
to obtain versions of one and the same article in a number
of different languages, usually in good and reliable translations. Useful, too, in a more limited sphere, can be equivalent patent specifications filed in various countries,
although it must be remembered here that many amend-
ments may have been made in the course of prosecution.
They are, however, particularly useful as a source of up-to-
date technical terms, often for new concepts. It is also useful
to remember that the claims of Finnish patent specifications
are also given in Swedish on the printed specifications.
Many of the bilingual official documents emanating from
such countries as Belgium, Switzerland, Canada and South
Africa can also be useful to the translator. Translations of
standard technical books into various languages are also
useful sources of information to the technical translator as
are the foreign-language versions of certain journals, particularly the "cover-to-cover" translations referred to
earlier in the book. The foreign-language summaries often
published in continental technical journals are, however,
frequently very poorly translated and are, therefore, not
reliable as sources. Foreign collections of books on a wide
range of subjects, such as the French *Que sais-je?* series or
the German *Sammlung Göschen*, can also be invaluable to
the translator wishing to acquaint himself with foreign
terminology in a given subject. The catalogues of mail
order firms can also be extremely useful as sources of correct
terminology, particularly in the quixotic and mercurial
sphere of fashion.

In a word, there are many reliable sources of information
available to the translator in his search for the right word
in the right place, and it is up to him to use his imagination
in hunting them out. It is also up to those training him to
make him aware of the possibilities. It is also assumed that
the translator will make full and appropriate use of foreign
radio broadcasts and that he will watch television pro-

grammes when abroad, since these sources can also be of
inestimable help to him in his work.

(c) Terminology services

As has been stated, dictionaries and glossaries are already
out of date before they appear. Added to this, new terms
are being coined daily, coupled to which there is far from
uniformity of terminology or nomenclature in many specialized fields. All these factors mean that the translator will
frequently encounter words in texts the meaning of which
it is quite impossible for him to discover or deduce from
the sources at his disposal. In such cases, he will consult
his colleagues working in similar fields, but if this too fails,
he may well consider the various terminology services
operating within the world of translators. Several linguistic
publications operate a terminology enquiry service for their
readers while some of the professional bodies catering for
translators have a similar facility. The only disadvantage
of these is that an answer will not necessarily be forthcom-
ing or, if it is, it may be incorrect and there will be a delay
in obtaining it. We shall be having more to say about this
problem in relation to computerized techniques in Chapter
VII.

From April 1959 until the end of 1969, the Metropolitan
New York Chapter of the American Medical Writers
Association published, with the support of the American
Translators Association, a publication called the *Translation
Inquirer*. This publication aimed at being of service to
translators in the fields of science and technology as well as
of literature by enabling them to consult a wide circle of
fellow-workers with respect to problems of both terminology
and style. It provided during its ten years or so of publication an excellent means for obtaining answers to many
queries. There is some likelihood that it will be continued,
perhaps in a slightly different form. The collected numbers

nevertheless still form a useful source of information for translators. The *Technical Translation Bulletin*, published by the Aslib Technical Translation Group, also has a regular terminology section through which members of the Group can endeavour to solve their problems. Likewise, the *T.G. Newsletter*, published by the Translators' Guild of the Institute of Linguists, has a section entitled *Word Change* which fulfils a similar function. The German language journal *Lebende Sprachen* operates a similar *Terminologiedienst*, as do some of the continental societies for translators.

These various services do not always provide all the answers, but they do provide some of them and translators should, therefore, be aware of their existence.

(d) *Linguistic journals*

There are today very many journals appearing in various parts of the world connected in one way or another with languages. Certain of these are concerned more specifically with translation, some of them being the journals of the member societies of the *Fédération Internationale des Traducteurs*, to which we referred in Chapter III. These include *Babel*, the Federation's own journal, the *Mitteilungsblatt für Dolmetscher und Übersetzer* published by the *Bundesverband der Dolmetcher and Ubersetzer e.V.*, one of the West German member societies, *Van Taal tot Taal*, the journal of the Dutch society and *Translatøren*, the journal of the Danish society. Reference has already been made to the *Technical Translation Bulletin* of the Aslib Technical Translation Group and the *Incorporated Linguist* of the Institute of Linguists. Reference has also already been made to the German journal *Lebende Sprachen*, noted for its lists of specialized terminology in various fields and also for its detailed criticisms of published translations.

All translators should read the journals catering for them

and their interests. Once again, it is obvious that few can
afford to subscribe to all of these, but they can all be consulted in the library of *CILT* (Centre for Information on
Language Teaching) in London. This is a government-
sponsored body catering primarily for the interests of
teachers of modern languages, although it also covers
many aspects of the field of interest to translators, including a
card index of linguistic research projects proceeding in this
country, some of which are of special interest to translators.
It also publishes *Language Teaching Abstracts* quarterly.

Most of the journals referred to are of interest to translators because of reviews of new dictionaries and glossaries,
terminology services and articles of general interest. Consequently, they too should form part of the translator's
regular reading material. There are also many linguistic
journals of peripheral interest to the translator, such as
those dealing with modern language teaching in general,
audio-visual aids and computerized techniques.

(e) *Colleagues*

No translator is omniscient, either linguistically or in
relation to subject matter, so that he need have no fear or
shame in admitting this either to his colleagues or to his
clients. Humility is, in fact, a very good ingredient in a
translator's personality. Most groups or associations of
translators hold meetings periodically, for example the
Aslib Technical Translation Group and the Translators'
Guild of the Institute of Linguists. At these members can
meet their colleagues, get to know them and "pick their
brains". This is all part of good professional relations, and
translators should take the opportunity of making the most
of facilities of this type offered to them. This is particularly
necessary since, although some problems are common to
all translators, each specific category has its own classes of
problems. There is much that could be done, for example

in the way of an exchange of ideas between technical and literary translators. At present, they tend to keep apart to a much greater extent perhaps than analogous groups within other professions. Exchange of ideas and their cross-fertilization are desirable amongst any group of people, more particularly those engaged in processing similar material. Much too can be gained from visits to colleagues' offices. No two translators or sections operate in exactly the same way, and much can be learnt from seeing how the other fellow works. You may well still prefer your own method, but at least you see another way of tackling similar problems. Translators, particularly those working for industrial firms, frequently consult one another by 'phone or telex on terminological problems too.

(f) *Lists of translators*

These are of use both to translators and to their clients—to the former should they wish to pass on work to other translators if it is outside their field of competence or if they wish to find a suitable translator for a specific language and subject-matter combination. There are two types of lists of translators, namely those that are published and those that are not published or which possibly have a restricted circulation. Amongst the published lists are those of the members of the Translators' Guild of the Institute of Linguists. This list is cross-indexed in a variety of ways, such that it is easily possible to find a translator of a given mother tongue specializing in a given subject who lives in a particular part of the country. This index has one advantage over many others in that the entries in it have been vetted by the committee of the Translators' Guild and that they have been based on an objective evaluation of the translators' capabilities. The Index is reprinted periodically, is kept up to date by supplements and is available to the public. Aslib keeps an unpublished Register of Specialist

Translators which was begun in the early thirties. It is available to Aslib members and at present contains the names of over 200 experienced translators who are subject specialists in the fields of science and technology and who have proved translating ability in various languages. Information on the translators is contained on punched feature cards and the Register is kept up to date by periodical questionnaires to the translators on it. Translators obtaining commissions through the Register pay a small commission to Aslib, if they are not members thereof in their own right. The chemical, physical and biological sciences are most fully covered in the Register, and between 400 and 500 enquiries for the services of translators from it are received annually. The Dutch Society of Translators (*Nederlands Genootschap van Vertalers*) has a printed list of its members, classified in much the same ways as the Index of the Translators' Guild. It too is reprinted periodically.

There are also various commercially produced lists of translators, all suffering, to a greater or lesser extent, from the shortcoming that the entries are based more or less entirely on information supplied by the translators themselves. This means that, in some cases, there are translators seemingly offering to undertake translations from and into up to six or more languages on a vast number of subjects! A volume entitled *Who's Who in Translating and Interpreting* was published in London in 1967. It gives personal details and linguistic capabilities of a wide number of translators, for the most part resident in the United Kingdom. Its method of classification nevertheless makes it difficult to use as a list for finding a translator for a specific commission. An *International Directory of Translators and Interpreters* was likewise published in London in 1967. It has a world coverage and is cross-indexed in various ways to enable one to find a suitable translator for a given requirement. It also contains useful notes on some of the national societies of translators. Another *Directory of Technical and*

Scientific Translators and Services was published in London in 1968. Once again, its coverage is for the most part restricted to translators resident in the United Kingdom. Unlike the other lists, it contains a section devoted to translation bureaux, as well as notes on marking up translations for the typist or printer and on costs of translations.

On the whole, it is better to find translators by personal recommendation rather than through any lists, and this certainly applies to finding translators from the classified sections of a telephone directory. Translators and translation bureaux are listed in such directories, but in this case the good are very likely to be indistinguishable from the bad.

(g) *Lists of Translations*

As we have already stated, the last thing any translator will wish to do is to translate again what has already been translated, this applying more particularly in the sphere of technical material for information purposes. Consequently, there are certain lists available of both published and unpublished translations which translators normally consult prior to starting an assignment.

Best known amongst these is probably the *Commonwealth Index of Unpublished Translations*. The Index was established in 1951 to serve as the British copy of the central index to English translations of scientific and technical literature from most languages centrally notified through the Commonwealth Scientific Liaison Office. The coverage has since been extended to all subjects and not only are single articles listed, but also journals of which a cover-to-cover translation exists in English. Some 220,000 items entered on cards are at present filed in the Index which is kept by Aslib in London. The Index represents information collected from over 200 libraries and information departments of private or nationalized industry, research establishments of all kinds, local authorities, universities and technical colleges. Anyone may use the Index, and in a year there are roughly 20,000 enquiries, more than 10% of which are satisfied. Enquirers are given the locations of translations and are expected to apply directly to the holding organization. It is important to note that this is purely an index of translations and that Aslib does not hold copies of translations. On the other hand, the National Lending Library, situated at Boston Spa in Yorkshire, which comes under the Department of Education and Science, does hold copies of translations. The facilities provided in the way of translations by the National Lending Library are quite extensive. The Library now holds over 150,000 translations of articles and books and these are currently being received in microfiche form from America at the rate of about 6,000 a year. The Library publishes a monthly *N.L.L. Translations Bulletin*, listing new acquisitions in this field. It also publishes a monthly *List of Books received from the USSR and Translated Books*. The Library also arranges the cover-to-cover translation into English of certain Russian journals, the translation of individual articles appearing in Russian journals, as well as sponsoring the translation of Russian books. Application should be made to the National Lending Library for details of these various services, many of which are not as well known as they deserve to be, particularly amongst translators.

The *World Index of Scientific Translations* is published by the European Translations Centre at Delft in the Netherlands. This Index is concerned primarily with indicating the location of translations from such languages as Arabic, Bulgarian, Chinese, Finnish, Hungarian, Japanese, Russian and other Slavonic languages into West European languages, primarily English, German and French. In this way, it is more akin to Aslib rather than the National Lending Library, in that it does not primarily set out to hold translations, but to indicate where they are held. The

National Lending Library is the British national centre for
the European Translations Centre.

It will thus be seen that there are many ways in which a
translator or an information officer can check whether a
translation of a given item already exists. It should also be
borne in mind that these indexes of translations have
arisen only through the co-operation of those preparing
translations or having them prepared. Consequently, it is
only through continued and further co-operation that they
can grow and thus become even more useful to those using
them. Many translations are obviously highly confidential
for a variety of reasons, but others, such as translations of
published articles or patent specifications, are not, and can
and should be notified, bearing in mind that it is not necessary to divulge the source of a translation to an enquirer if
it is desired to keep this confidential. In such cases, the
holder of the index will act as intermediary.

(h) *Typewriters*

Many translators do their own typing, at least in so far
as drafts of publication translations and information translations are concerned. For such work, a typewriter intermediate in size between a small portable and a full-size
office machine is preferable, since it is more robust than the
former and easier to handle than the latter. A typewriter
of intermediate size can also be used for producing stencils
should this be desired. It can be an advantage to the translator to have a typewriter with a longer than normal carriage
for taking wider paper, this sometimes being useful for
dealing with the reproduction of tables, etc. If the translator is dealing with material to be translated into foreign
languages, it is essential that he should have fitted to his
machine and that of his typist the appropriate accents and
signs. Few things look worse than accents and signs inserted
in pencil or ink on an otherwise immaculately presented

F

translation. It is, however, surprising how many translators overlook this seemingly elementary point. Similarly, translators should also remember that typewriter ribbons wear out and that it is possible to clean the keys of a typewriter. If a few accents only are required, it is most convenient to have the fraction keys removed and the accents added in their place as so-called "dead" keys. This means that the accent is typed first, then the letter, the carriage moving along only when the second key has been struck. Devices are available which enable special signs, such as letters of the Greek alphabet or certain mathematical symbols, to be fitted to the typewriter as required. There are also interchangeable keyboard units and so-called "golf-balls" for specific languages that can be fitted to electric typewriters, all of which can be useful to the translator or his typist. Small sub- and super-script figures can be useful for typing chemical and mathematical formulae. It is likewise easy to convert a typewriter for "chemical" typing by adapting the right-hand shift lock key into what might be called a "half shift key". This enables formulae such as H_2SO_4 to be typed easily. It is also possible to obtain special correction ribbons and papers which obviate the need to use an eraser. Translators should also remember that A4 paper is now used almost universally on the continent and to an increasing extent in this country.

Should translators be preparing material for publication in foreign languages, which will be set and printed in this country, it is as well to know that there are certain printers specializing in this kind of work who hold large stocks of various foreign-language types.

(i) *Dictating machines*

There is on the market for translators requiring them a very wide range of dictating machines based on discs, wire and tape, with all manner of accessories for erasing, playing back, etc. For speech work, a reasonably small, if not completely portable machine is preferable and also one that has a reasonable playing time. Machines with only a 10-minute playing time are not really suitable for a translator, since few translations other than commercial letters can be dictated within this time. A visit to a tape recorder centre or a supplier of office machines will be useful before deciding on a given piece of equipment.

(j) *Photocopying machines*

Free-lance translators or translation bureaux that wish to offer their clients a comprehensive service should also have a photocopying machine of some type available. Once again, there are many to choose from, and manufacturers of such equipment should be consulted. Mention of photocopies reminds us again that translators should always be provided with perfect photocopies from which to work, particularly in the case of languages not using the Roman alphabet, such as Arabic and Japanese. Special care should in any case be taken to ensure that the margins are clear if photocopies are being made from a bound volume. These may seem pedantic or minor points, but much time can be lost in puzzling over a word or letter that has been reproduced indistinctly in a photocopy. The same applies to small figures in tables.

(k) *Office furniture*

Amongst the office furniture that translators may find useful are a desk with pull-out flaps on which he can place his dictionaries, etc., a stand for the document on which he is working, a revolving bookcase for housing his reference books and a suitably positioned good lamp, possibly of the angle-poise variety. Needless to say, the translator should also have a quiet room in which to work, since his activity requires concentration and freedom from interruption. Should more than one translator using a typewriter be working in the same office, it is advisable that this should be of the "silent" variety.

READING LIST

Cook-Radmore, D. A. J.—*Indexes of Translators*. The Incorporated Linguist, January 1969, pp. 13-15.

Finlay, I. F.—*The Translators' Tools of Trade*. Aslib Technical Translation Bulletin, Vol. 14, No. 3, December 1968, pp. 96-100.

Flegon, A. (compiler)—*Who's Who in Translating and Interpreting*. London 1967.

Gullberg, I. E.—*Some Notes on Dictionaries and Dictionary-Making*. Babel, Vol. XI, No. 4 1965, pp. 168-174.

Hamel, G. A.—*Translations—Their Collection and Indexing*. Babel, Vol. XII, No. 2 1966, pp. 84-86.

Holloway, A. H.—*Tools of the Trade*. Aslib Technical Translation Bulletin, Vol. 9, No. 1, March 1963, pp. 4-14.

Millard, P. (compiler)—*Directory of Technical and Scientific Translators & Services*. London 1968.

Pond, B.—*International Directory of Translators and Interpreters*. London 1967.

Vries, L. de—*Making a Technical Dictionary*. Babel, Vol. II, No. 4, December 1956, pp. 159-162.

Tybulewicz, A.—*Cover-to-Cover Translations of Soviet Journals*. Aslib Proceedings, Vol. 22, No. 2, 1970, pp. 55-62.

CHAPTER VII

THE TRANSLATOR AND COMPUTERIZED TECHNIQUES

During the past twenty years or so, there have been outstanding advances in electronics and in techniques relying for their operation on the use of minute electrical components. These have resulted, amongst other things, in equipment referred to as computers which are, in many cases, capable of performing highly complicated operations and calculations which previously took human beings several hundred times as long. Many modern achievements, such as automatic telephone exchanges and landings on the moon, would have been impossible without such techniques.

This vast development in computers also gave rise to the suggestion that it might be possible to use them for making translations, the general term used for activities in this field being "machine translation" or M.T. for short. Research groups were set up in various countries, including Great Britain, Russia, the U.S.A. and Italy, in the late fifties and early sixties for the purpose of investigating these possibilities. A group at the University of London concerned itself more particularly with the problems involved in translating French into English, while most of the work carried out in the United States was concerned with the translation of Russian into English. An international conference on the machine translation of languages and applied language analysis was held at the National Physical Laboratory at Teddington in September 1961, at which a variety of papers was presented by research-workers from many countries. It is clear from a perusal of the titles of these papers that machine translation is obviously a field in which languages as most of us understand them have merged with such other disciplines as statistics, electronics, mathematics together with an admixture of logic. Although much of the research into machine translation seems remote from everyday linguistic activities, it has had its influence on, and benefits to, various aspects of possibly more practical linguistic spheres through such matters as the structural analysis of languages and the preparation of statistical word-counts of typical texts in various languages—these latter being most useful for training purposes. One of the difficulties surrounding the subject of machine translation is, in common with most relatively new spheres of investigation, the completely new jargon which has been created to explain some of the activities involved in it. Terms such as transfer grammar, semantic message detection, distributional classes and logical trees will mean little to the conventional linguist. The same position has in fact arisen in relation to the general science of linguistics in recent years. The two main difficulties to be overcome in machine translation are those presented by the multiple meanings of words and by differences in word order. The former have in their time given rise to certain frivolous examples of alleged machine translations, although the impact of these has been weakened a little over the years.

The world's first manned space flight by the Russian Yuri Gagarin in April 1961 provided a great impetus for research into the possibilities of providing machine translations of Russian technical literature into English. This event brought to the attention of the scientific world at large the fact that Russia was a power to be reckoned with in relation to the many branches of science and technology involved in this achievement and that it was, therefore, desirable to be able to make available the results of her efforts in various fields. Most of the research on machine translation was therefore, in America in particular, directed towards this aim.

I do not propose to consider here the technical problems of machine translation, but merely to point out that in all such work it is necessary to prepare or pre-edit a text for feeding into a computer, which is in this context really a dictionary which is able to sift through the possible meanings and functions of a word in a given context, and likewise to post-edit the result produced by the computer.

The general net result of the vast amount of research that has been carried out on machine translation throughout the world is that this method can be used, with the pre-editing referred to above, for the translating of technical or scientific texts in the information sphere, at least to the extent that their general interest can be evaluated and that a decision can then be made as to whether a more refined version should be produced by a human translator. Although the actual processing time in the computer is small, the preparation and final editing of the result have to be taken into account, as have also the preparation of the dictionary and the cost of the computer time. Unless such machine translating were to be carried out on a national scale, it would be unlikely to prove an economic proposition. Certain of the centres previously working on machine translation have gradually tailed off their efforts in recent years, so that even information translators in the technical field need not feel excessively worried about their livelihoods, at least for the next few decades. There was, of course, never any serious intention that machine translation should invade the literary sphere, so that it would seem that translators in general can rest assured that they will not in the near future be supplanted by machines. An interesting marginal linguistic use of the computer is the generation of words of a specific consonant/vowel sequence for consideration as trade marks. This exercise was carried out a few years ago by a British firm, the computer being directed to produce a series of words on the pattern of "Kodak" and "Banlon". Certain of the results were highly interesting and some were unprintable!

Another sphere in which computers can and do have a very much more useful and immediate role to play in the sphere of translating lies in the direction of setting up a dictionary within a computer. Successful attempts have already been made in this field in Luxembourg and West Germany. These machines operate in such a way that, if a word or expression is fed into them, they will produce the appropriate translation of that word or expression within the given context in the target language. This is certainly a great aid to the translator who would, for example, be very pleased to be able to survey at a glance, as it were, the meaning given in all his dictionaries and glossaries for a specific term in a foreign language assuming, of course, that it was included in them. It would, in fact, be primarily the words and expressions within a given subject field which had not yet found their way into dictionaries that such computerized dictionaries would ideally contain. A preliminary survey has been carried out in Great Britain by the Atomic Energy Research Establishment at Harwell, with the support of the Office for Scientific and Technical Information, to assess the likely use of such a facility in the United Kingdom.

Many translators remain very sceptical of all these modern developments, in much the same way as some teachers of modern languages do in relation to the various audio-visual aids now available to them. Some of these rather short-sighted views, even if they are understandable, savour of the proud boast of a nineteenth-century producer of language books, namely that what he was teaching was grammar, not languages! We all make use of many things that modern science and technology have provided for us, ranging from drip-dry shirts to transistor radios, and it would be foolish not to make use of any linguistic aids if they can make us more efficient and productive assuming, of course, that we can make suitable use of the additional time placed at our disposal as a result. The various more conventional tools of trade of the translator discussed in detail in the previous chapter have improved immeasurably in quality and quantity over the past two decades, thus rendering most translators more efficient and productive, and it seems likely that computerized techniques, at least on the level of dictionaries, will likewise do so in the next two decades. Hence, gratitude rather than scepticism would seem to be the appropriate reaction.

READING LIST

Arthern, P. J.—*An Electronic Dictionary*. The Incorporated Linguist, January 1967, pp. 70-72.

Babel—Vol. II, No. 3, October 1956 (special issue devoted to Machine Translation of Languages).

Booth, A. D.—*Machine Translation—A Challenge to the Linguist*. The Incorporated Linguist, April 1962, pp. 34-41.

Delavenay, E.—*An Introduction to Machine Translation*. London 1960.

Sykes, J. B.—*Computerized Dictionaries*. Aslib Technical Translation Bulletin, Vol. 14, No. 1, Spring 1968, pp. 17-20.

Szanser, A. J.—*Machine Translation at the National Physical Laboratory, Teddington*. The Incorporated Linguist, October 1966, pp. 102-109.

Szanser, A. J.—*Machine Translation, the Evaluation of an Experiment*. The Incorporated Linguist, October 1967, pp. 90-95.

CHAPTER VIII

THE BUSINESS SIDE OF TRANSLATING

Many professional people do not have a very highly developed business sense, often to their own cost and that of their clients. Translating, in common with other professions, has its business side, and this applies more particularly to free-lance translators working for a variety of clients, many of whom may not be based in the United Kingdom. It is consequently up to all translators to ensure that they operate their practices on proper business-like principles since, if they do not, they are more than likely not to prosper in the long run.

There are many aspects to the successful running of a translating practice from the point of view of a business, not the least of which is reliability. This implies that the translator must provide his various clients, both major and minor, with a reliable service in relation to accuracy, presentation, charges and delivery dates. On the other hand, it is also incumbent on the customer or client to treat his translator in a responsible manner, not making impossible or unreasonable demands on him in relation to such matters as delivery dates. There are very many cases in which the translator is expected to be the fastest-working link in a long production chain, being compressed, as it were, between the original author and the printer. It is true that many translators, even those working for publication, can work extremely quickly, producing up to 5,000 words a day or more, but working under pressure in this way is hardly likely to be conducive to the production of their best work, even on the information level. Consequently, planning ahead and allowing the translator a reasonable time in which to produce his best work are important elements in customer education. Likewise, customers should not make unreasonable demands on translators in relation to working outside their language or subject-matter specializations. After all, you would not go to an ear, nose and throat specialist to have your appendix removed, and you should not, by the same token, expect an expert in electrical engineering to be able to cope adequately with a text relating to the dyeing of wool.

Translators should also ensure that their book-keeping and accounting give a professional impression. Accounts scrawled on any old piece of paper are hardly likely to inspire confidence any more than are translations typed with a worn-out ribbon or those with accents put in by hand in pencil. Free-lance translators should preferably have their own letter-heads, account forms and compliment slips. They must behave in a professional manner if they wish to be regarded and treated as members of a profession. A quotation from Goethe's *Faust* seems not inappropriate in this context: *Was du ererbt von deinen Vätern hast, erwirb es, um es zu besitzen.* Most translators working full-time on a free-lance basis will find it advisable to employ a professional accountant to deal with their income tax, the few guineas a year this costs being more than amply compensated for by the expert advice the accountant will be able to give concerning the many allowances that are available to the self-employed free-lance. It is, therefore, essential that the translator keeps proper books and accounts as well as records and evidence of expenses incurred in carrying out his profession. This is not difficult; it is merely necessary to develop orderly habits in this direction. Another important point is that a free-lance translator and a translation bureau should not be under-capitalized, since some clients, particularly certain large firms, take rather a long time to pay their accounts. Likewise, translators of books will very often not be paid advances on their fee, so that they may well be working for a number of months before they receive any money from a publisher. It is unfair on the part of a translating bureau, for example, to keep translators waiting for their fee merely because it itself has to wait to be paid by its client. Many free-lance translators will, however, find that they are at any one time owed quite large sums, amounting in some cases to several hundred pounds, and this they must be able to carry. In the case of large agencies, this figure may well run into several thousand pounds, so the need for sufficient capital becomes evident.

Certain clients and agencies occasionally ask prospective translators to provide sample translations free of charge. This is a practice prohibited by all professional bodies of translators, and rightly so, since it is analogous to going to a dental surgeon and saying "please extract this third molar and, if you do it to my satisfaction, you may then extract the second molar too, but if I am not satisfied with the first extraction, I shall go elsewhere for the second one." The only occasion on which free sample translations should be provided is if a translator has been short-listed for a post and is to be given a test, which is a very wise practice for all concerned.

How do translators charge for their work? There are various methods operating in different countries. It will be most convenient to consider first the system generally operating in Great Britain. The minimum fees to be charged for translations are based for the most part on those recommended by the Institute of Linguists for its members, these being reviewed periodically at meetings of the members of its Translators' Guild. For the purpose of assessing fees, languages have been classified into various groups, their position in a given group being based on such factors as: the absolute degree of difficulty of the language in question for an English-speaking person, the availability of translators from the language, the availability of technical aids to translation, such as dictionaries and other reference books, and the relative wordage used by the language to express a given thought or text. These factors, expressed in the form of a formula, result in Spanish receiving a value of 1, while Russian receives a value of 2. At the top end of the scale, Turkish has a value of 4·8, exceeding only Finnish and Hungarian, with a value of 3·9 each, in this respect. The application of this principle has resulted in the formation of four groups covering the main European languages. For example, French, Italian and Spanish are in Group I, such languages as Afrikaans, Danish, German and Portuguese in Group II, Russian, Icelandic and the Celtic languages are in Group III, while Group IV contains such languages as Estonian, Finnish, Hungarian and Turkish. Fees are based on the number of words in the original text, normally being quoted in units of 1,000 or "kilowords". The fees are further quoted for non-specialized and specialized texts both into and from English, and a suitable increase is made for specialized work and for that to be translated out of English. This results in a scale of fees such that a translation from Hungarian will, for example, cost roughly three times that of a translation from French.

Japanese and Chinese have been placed in a separate group, and fees for translations from these languages are based on the number of characters in the original text. Chinese texts contain characters of one type only whereas, as we have seen, Japanese texts, particularly those of a technical nature, will contain both Chinese characters and examples of the two different sets of *kana* or syllabaries. The concept of a "word" as applied to western European languages is foreign to Japanese, but it has been found that, in a technical text, there are likely to be two and a half characters or symbols to each Japanese "word".

Over and above these basic fees, there are various surcharges for priority work, translations required for publication (where proof-reading may also be involved), as well as for advertising material. The preparation of translations of slogans and advertising copy is a highly specialized field, and is often one in which the co-operation of a translator and a copywriter is desirable. It is also a highly important field for advertisers, since a good slogan or advertisement can do much in the way of increasing sales of the goods in question. Even such a simple slogan as "Cool as a Mountain Stream" can hardly be translated literally into various foreign languages without losing some of its original impact and psychological overtones! Consequently, translations of slogans and advertising copy can be very expensive compared with the number of words involved.

The scale of minimum fees recommended by the Institute of Linguists does not apply to the translation of books for publishers. In this case, there are recommended fees suggested by the Translators' Association of the Society of Authors. These are quoted for fiction and general non-fiction and for specialized non-fiction, with or without royalties by negotiation. These fees are normally lower than those recommended by the Institute of Linguists and tend not to differ according to the language from which the translation is made, although the law of supply and demand obviously plays a certain role here too. It should be mentioned that there is normally a royalty payment, based on the number of performances, to translators of works for the stage.

As has already been mentioned, translators working for translation bureaux normally receive two-thirds of the fee paid by the client to the bureau, although in some cases the bureau will retain much more than one-third of the fee paid by the client, particularly if the translation has to be edited or retyped.

Fees for translations often shock those requiring them.

Admittedly, some translators do charge excessively high fees, while some charge excessively low fees. There is no direct correlation between the quality of a translation and the fee charged for it. All that can be said is that bad translations are always too expensive and that a well-produced, accurate translation is worth the fee charged for it. Reliability, too, is a rare enough quality in this modern world, so that it can be worth paying for.

As we have said, translation fees in the United Kingdom are based on the number of words in original text, which seems an eminently logical basis, since it is, after all, the text that is processed by the translator, and such matters as the excessive length of words in German have already been taken into account in the assigning of that language to a specific group. Various continental countries do, however, use different methods for assessing fees. In some, the translation fee is based on the number of words in the translation, while in others the fee is based on the number of lines of a specific length in the translation (frequently based on a given number of strokes of the typewriter). Similarly, many continental countries do not differentiate between source languages when assessing the fee. The thinking behind this is that a translator should not really expect to be paid more because he has chosen to study Finnish rather than Portuguese. There is, in fact, much to be said for this view which is, as we have said, often applied in relation to the translation of books for publishers in the United Kingdom.

Fees for translations differ considerably from country to country, although not from one part of a country to another. Thus, translations are not really more expensive if obtained in London than they are if obtained in Manchester or Glasgow. The level of fees depends on such factors as the general cost of living in a country, the extent to which translators have established themselves as a professional body and the degree to which a country is, as a whole, "translation conscious". For example, fees for translations are in Spain much lower than in the United Kingdom, while those in Sweden are considerably higher than those in the United Kingdom.

Fees for Conference translators or revisers are laid down by the *Association Internationale des Traducteurs de Conférence* (A.I.T.C.) and are normally quoted on a daily basis.

There is a very wide spectrum of salaries paid to translators working on a full-time basis in British industry. Salaries range from about £1000 to £3000 per annum, depending on such factors as age, languages covered and degree of responsibility. Full-time, free-lance translators are likely to earn anything from £2000 to £4000 per annum. It will, therefore, be seen that salaries and incomes of professional translators compare reasonably favourably with those of their colleagues in other professions, although it must be admitted that translators working in industry are unlikely to rise to high managerial levels. By the nature of the service they provide they must, as it were, expand or extend horizontally rather than vertically, justifying increases in salary and status by providing a full linguistic service rather than purely a translating one. This is in fact occurring to an increasing extent as firms realize that the translator, as a professional linguist, can do very much more than merely translate.

Nevertheless, as stated at the beginning of this chapter, translators must behave as professionals if they wish others to treat them as such. Instances of unprofessional advertising, vast overcharging or undercutting and encroachment still occur, and these, coupled with various other examples of unprofessional behaviour, tend to denigrate the professional image of the translator. This is one of the reasons why translators should belong to their professional organizations and in this way make a corporate effort to improve their general position within the community.

READING LIST

Cave, S. C.—*Survey of Overseas Translation Rates*. The Incorporated Linguist, January 1967, pp. 12-19.

Finlay, I. F.—*Translators' Guild Remuneration Survey 1963*. The Incorporated Linguist, April 1964, pp. 38-40.

Finlay, I. F.—*Translators' Guild Remuneration Survey 1966*. The Incorporated Linguist, July 1967, pp. 70-72.

Sykes, J. B.—*Taxation of Translators*. The Incorporated Linguist, October 1966, pp. 110-112.

CHAPTER IX

TRANSLATOR TRAINING

As in most other spheres, the trained translator is, other things being equal, more likely to be a good practitioner, at least at an earlier stage in his career, than the one who has not been trained. This fact has been taken into account on the Continent for a very much longer period of time than it has in this country, although the position here has changed immeasurably over the past ten years or so.

Most translators working in the United Kingdom today who are over forty probably more or less drifted into translating from a variety of backgrounds, the common factor to which was a knowledge of or ability in languages other than their language of habitual use. Many are modern languages graduates from the language and literature type of course available at most universities. Others had acquired their knowledge of languages through circumstances of birth or education, while others will have acquired their linguistic knowledge through periods in the Services or travel. Although many of these translators bring to their work an excellent linguistic and subject-matter background, there are few of them who would not perhaps, on reflexion, admit that some of the time spent in their education, particularly at university level, could have been spent more profitably if they had at that time known that they were to become translators or if there had at that time been a specific course of training for translators. Many translators practising today in the scientific and technical field once had an excellent knowledge of such subjects as Gothic,

Middle High German, Church Slavonic or Romance philo-
logy which, interesting and useful as it might be, can
hardly compare with a knowledge of basic engineering
principles as a useful ingredient in their education for the
kind of work they are now doing.

This realization that training for translators should be
more vocational in character and that there should be an
attempt towards interdisciplinary training has in the past
few years, following upon continental models of many
years' standing, led to the establishment of various diploma
and degree courses, mainly at the newer universities, combining linguistic and subject-matter training as a basis for
future translators and, to a lesser extent, interpreters.
Results have already shown that such persons are, in general,
much better equipped to be recruited as junior translators
than those who have had a training purely in language and
literature.

Although these courses of training are constantly being
modified or added to, it will be useful to consider some of
those being offered at present. Amongst those with a distinct
linguistic bias rather than those in which a language is, as
it were, grafted on to a course basically devoted to non-
linguistic disciplines, is the post-graduate diploma in language studies at the Bath University of Technology. This
is a one-year course in French and German or Russian or
Spanish covering such matters as techniques of interpreting,
documentary translation and conference précis-writing,
together with international politics and aspects of science
and technology. Bath University of Technology also offers
a B.Sc. degree course in engineering with French, which
involves a period of industrial training in France. Bradford
Technical College offers two two-year courses, one for
translators and interpreters, the other for foreign corre-
spondents. The former course is available in German,
French, Russian, Spanish and Italian, and covers such
matters as scientific, technical, political, economic and com-

mercial subjects with a thoroughly developed knowledge of one major European language. The course also includes regional studies and training for interpreting at business and professional meetings. Attendance at a summer language school abroad during the first long vacation is also involved. The foreign correspondent course at Bradford covers French, German, Spanish, Russian and Italian and deals with such matters as languages, shorthand, typewriting and secretarial practice, together with commerce, more particularly as it applies to the woollen and other export trades of the region. The University of Bradford offers a four-year honours B.A. course in French, German, Russian or Spanish involving the study of two languages, modern European thought and literature, as well as science, technology and general linguistics. The third year of the course is spent abroad. Ealing Technical College offers a four-year honours B.A. course in applied language studies covering three languages, background studies, interpreting and translating. Here, too, the third year is spent abroad. Holborn College of Law, Languages and Commerce offers a number of courses in this field, the most interesting of which is a post-graduate Diploma in general and technical translating, lasting six months. The languages involved are French and German or Spanish. Such matters as translation and terminology in engineering, nuclear physics, atomic energy, industrial chemistry, automation, electronics and mining are covered, in addition to which the course also includes social and institutional studies. There is emphasis on techniques rather than specialized subject spheres. Holborn also offers a three-year Diploma in foreign languages and related social studies. Courses of much the same type as those outlined above are also available at Leeds Polytechnic, the University of Salford (a course very similar to that at the University of Bradford), the University of Surrey and the Wolverhampton College of Technology.

Courses involving basically technical degrees with the addition of one language are available at the University of Birmingham and the University of East Anglia, while the University of Surrey offers an honours degree course in Russian language and Soviet studies.

This by no means completes the list of such possibilities, since new courses of one type or another are being developed every year. Those interested in such courses should consult the various publications giving up-to-date details of courses.

A particularly interesting development is an intensive course in reading Japanese which started at the University of Sheffield in 1970. This course, initially of two months' duration, sets out to teach the ability to read Japanese within a given subject sphere. The teaching method is based on one practised at the University of Prague. Bearing in mind the great shortage of translators from Japanese and of scientists who can read this language, translators are particularly interested in the way in which this course will develop. It is a very good example of the use of languages for special purposes, and many linguists hope that it will be the first of many such courses setting out to impart to translators and others purely a translating or reading ability in a given language within a given set of related subjects, since there is a great need for people having this ability. The reading courses in French, German and Russian attended by many senior science graduates have never proved remarkably successful in this regard.

As has been pointed out, the majority of the courses referred to above sets out to combine a knowledge of languages with that of various other subjects, so that the final graduate has, as it were, a foot in at least two camps. We already saw in Chapter I that such combined knowledge is essential on the part of the scientific or technical translator. Also, as was seen from Chapter VI, there are many things other than purely linguistic and subject-matter knowledge which enter into the comprehensive ability of a translator. Certain of these, but not all, are also covered in the courses of training referred to above. There is a very great danger in some of these courses that the training will be too theoretical and divorced from the practical working conditions and milieu of the translator. This is one reason why those in charge of such training courses should, ideally, have had practical experience as translators. Another way of overcoming this difficulty is for undergraduates to visit the translating sections or departments of large firms in order to see translators at work. Much confusion in education today arises from the gap between theory and practice, and anything that can be done to narrow or eliminate this gap is highly desirable.

Most of the longer courses of training referred to involve a period of study in the country in which the language being studied is spoken, a requisite also for most students for honours degrees in modern-language courses of the more conventional language and literature type. Many of the courses require the preparation of an extended essay on an aspect of the country of the student's choice and, as has been seen, general background studies of the country, these being of immense benefit to the translator in his work.

Although no general course of training should be too restrictive, there is everything to be gained from pruning the material to be studied to that which is applicable to the aim in view. Consequently, skills not required can be omitted and use can be made of such aids as word frequency counts of the languages and disciplines involved. Equally, material used for training should aim to simulate that which will be encountered in practice. This involves the various categories of material referred to in Chapter III. Courses of training should also familiarize the student with all the literature and subject-matter aids available in the languages involved. There is even much to be said for allowing the use of dictionaries in examinations, in order to simulate practical working conditions as far as possible.

Students should also be encouraged to read critically as many published translations as they can, comparing them with the originals. Careful study of such masterpieces as R. Queneau's *Exercises de style*, which has also been translated into English, can also be of inestimable value.

In addition to the various courses in translating considered above, it should also be pointed out that the Institute of Linguists has for the past few years offered a translator option in its highest level examinations. The successful passing of this final examination does not imply that the candidate can then automatically regard himself as a fully fledged translator, any more than can the graduates from the courses referred to above. It merely implies that such persons can be considered with confidence for posts as junior translators. It is important to realize that on-the-job training is as important for translators as for any other type of graduate. Nevertheless, a translator who has also been given a general training in scientific principles is better equipped to enter industry as such than one who brings with him purely a knowledge of Molière and Racine.

The importance of refresher courses and of periodical visits to the countries of his source languages is also something that should be considered for translators of several years' standing. Although it is too much to hope for that translators be granted periods of sabbatical leave, there is much to be said for providing the opportunity for occasional visits abroad. Useful results can also come from exchanges of translators, for example in the case of English firms having overseas subsidiaries or associates. Translators can stagnate if they work for too long in a vacuum.

There is sometimes much discussion as to whether it is better to take a linguist and train him in technical disciplines in order that he might become a translator, or whether it is not better to take a scientist and teach him languages in order that he might become a translator. The nature of the courses referred to above suggests that it is better still to train a person concurrently in both languages and general scientific principles. Nevertheless, of the two extreme alternatives, it is considered better to take a linguist and graft on to him the principles and terminology of a given technical sphere rather than to take an expert in the technical sphere and teach him languages to the degree required. After all, languages are, in the final analysis, the basic material or medium processed by the translator rather than the subject-matter they are used to communicate, and it is more important that the language of the original be understood than the subject-matter although, ideally, the knowledge of the one should be commensurate with the knowledge of the other, this being the aim of modern courses of training for technical translators.

READING LIST

Bakaya, R. M.—*An Experiment in Compiling a Minimal Vocabulary for Reading Scientific-Technical Literature in Russian.* Babel, Vol. XIII, No. 3, 1967, pp. 163-168.

Committee on Research and Development in Modern Languages, First Report. Her Majesty's Stationery Office 1968.

Coveney, J.—*The Bath University Postgraduate Diploma in Language Studies.* The Incorporated Linguist, October 1969, pp. 88-90.

Languages for Special Purposes. CILT Reports and Papers 1. London 1969.

Sager, J. C.—*The Salford Course for Translators and Interpreters.* Aslib Technical Translation Bulletin, Vol. 10, No. 2, Summer 1964, pp. 93-104.

CHAPTER X

THE NEXT STEP

It has been the aim of this book to consider all the many aspects of the translating scene and to refer, however briefly, to all facets of the profession of translating. Consequently, very little remains to be said in this short concluding chapter.

Should you feel, after having read the book and the various works in the reading lists at the end of each chapter, that you would like to penetrate further into the world of translating, assuming you have the necessary temperamental qualities and other characteristics desirable for doing so, then I should suggest that you try to meet some professional translators, talk to them, see how they work, find out the kind of lives they lead and what financial and other rewards they derive from their work. Equally well, you should read as many translations of all types, styles and periods as you can, comparing them with the originals as and when possible and practicable. If you feel that you would like to study to become a translator, examine very carefully the various courses available, study the advertisements for translators appearing in the press in order to see what qualifications are being asked for, what salaries and possibilities of promotion are being offered. In other words, try to immerse yourself as far as possible in the world of translators and translating and then make your decision.

Finally, a gentle word of warning is perhaps appropriate. It is this: there is at present what one might be excused for calling a linguistic bandwagon. Languages in one form or another are being publicized to a much greater extent than ever before and, in some cases, courses are being offered which purport to impart a knowledge of and ability at them in seemingly record time with little expense and even less effort. The same might be said also of certain spheres in the world of music. There are those who can with a few chords on a guitar and a pretence at singing command fantastic success and acclaim, often of very short duration, while there are others who consider it only dignified to study and practise for years before confronting the public with the results of their labours. This also applies in the world of languages and in that of translating. Translating is a fine, interesting and well-paid career today, but in order to be amongst the top practitioners one needs to study long and hard and not to run before one can walk. Many mediocre translators have done very well in the past few years, but the ranks of the profession are rapidly consolidating, and it is unlikely that those who are not amongst the better and best will be able to survive in years to come.

Since this has been a book about an aspect of languages, I feel we cannot do better than close it with three quotations, the first from Latin, the second from Goethe's *Italienische Reise* and the third from Arabic. They are: *Verba volant, scripta manent*, meaning "Words vanish, what is written remains": *In der Kunst ist das Beste gut genug*, meaning "In art, the best is good enough", and:

وما من كاتب الّا سيفنى

ويبقى الدهر ما كتبت يداه

فلا تكتب بكفك غير شيء

يسرك في القيامة ان تراه

meaning "There is no writer but he shall pass away, while time will keep alive what his hands have written. So let not your hand write anything but what it will please you to see on the Day of Resurrection."

APPENDIX

List of relevant organizations and bodies

Aslib, 3 Belgrave Square, London, S.W.1.

Association Internationale des Traducteurs de Conférence (A.I.T.C.), 24 Avenue Krieg, Geneva, Switzerland.

British Standards Institution, British Standards House, 2 Park Street, London, W.1.

Fédération Internationale des Traducteurs (F.I.T.), 185 Avenue Victor Hugo, Paris XVI.

Institute of Linguists, 91 Newington Causeway, London, S.E.1.

International P.E.N., Glebe House, 62-63 Glebe Place, London, S.W.3.

National Lending Library, Boston Spa, Yorkshire.

Translators' Association, 84 Drayton Gardens, London, S.W.10.